ONLINE BRAND SUPREMO

Social Brand Marketing

10 Steps to Establish Your Brand on Facebook Quickly and Effectively.

First published by Online Brand Supremo 2019

Copyright © 2019 by Online Brand Supremo

All rights reserved. No part of this publication may be reproduced, stored or transmitted in any form or by any means, electronic, mechanical, photocopying, recording, scanning, or otherwise without written permission from the publisher. It is illegal to copy this book, post it to a website, or distribute it by any other means without permission.

Online Brand Supremo asserts the moral right to be identified as the author of this work.

Online Brand Supremo has no responsibility for the persistence or accuracy of URLs for external or third-party Internet Websites referred to in this publication and does not guarantee that any content on such Websites is, or will remain, accurate or appropriate.

Designations used by companies to distinguish their products are often claimed as trademarks. All brand names and product names used in this book and on its cover are trade names, service marks, trademarks and registered trademarks of their respective owners. The publishers and the book are not associated with any product or vendor mentioned in this book. None of the companies referenced within the book have endorsed the book.

First edition

This book was professionally typeset on Reedsy.
Find out more at reedsy.com

Getting Likes	65
Generate Quality Content	66
Step 8: Facebook Ads	68
Basics of Facebook Advertising	69
Creating a Page Like Ad	70
Creating Audiences	70
Creating Facebook Ads	71
Video Ads	72
Reports	73
Get a Custom Advertising Plan	74
Promote Your Business Locally	75
Promote Your Page	76
Promote Your Website	76
Get More Leads	77
Chapter Five: Delivering Value to Audience and Growing your...	79
Step 9 : Posting Relevancy and Quality	79
Use Emotions	82
Don't Overdo It	82
Keep Posts Short & Specific	83
Visual	83
Informational or Interesting	84
Apps for Business Marketing	85
Custom Tab Apps	85
Email capture apps	85
Quiz and Poll apps	86
Automatic Posting apps	86
Social Media Integration apps	87
Contest apps	87
Chapter Six: Monetizing your Business	88
Step 10 : Selling on Facebook	88

Don't Overdo It	91
Emphasize Use	91
Provide a Price Range	92
Heighten the Fear (of Missing Out)	93
Amp It Up	94
Facebook Groups	95
How to join a group?	95
Conclusion	97
References	98
A message from the Author	99
About the Author	100

Free Bonus!

As a thank you for purchasing this book we want to give you a **Free Bonus**. A info-graphic blueprint on how to start your online brand effectively. this will help you establish a business plan and tackle every element that is a necessity for your business one step at a time. whether you are using Facebook, Instagram, or any other platform for to establishing your presence. the steps in this amazing FREE info-graphic makes it easy to keep you in check all the time.

https://onlinebrandsupremo.com/infograph

Introduction

I would like to begin by thanking you for choosing this book, '*Social Brand Marketing: 10 steps to establish your brand on Facebook quickly and effectively*', and I hope you find this in interesting and informative in your quest to understanding social media marketing on one of its most popular platforms – Facebook.

Today, Facebook is one of the most popular social networking websites in the world. Many people believe that it's just to look for friends and be 'social,' but since a huge part of the world interacts on it, it's also for businesses who want to increase their reach.

The original purpose of Facebook was to connect people on the basis of their likes and interests; however, it later became monetized as it's a goldmine for companies who want to sell their products to consumers. With Facebook, you can easily get access to the likes, interests and even personal lives of your customers. Therefore, years after its founding, Facebook has become all about marketing and studying the people on it in order to sell products to them.

Facebook is an opportunity that you cannot miss, as you can reach out to millions of potential consumers without spending a lot of money on it. Nowadays, having a Facebook presence is essential for any brand that's trying to establish itself. Your product and work ethic might be great, but social media can make or break your idea or company.

At times, marketing on Facebook can be complex because to be successful at it, you need to know the whole thing inside out. The aim of this book is to familiarize you with all the necessary tricks and tips. You'll learn how to research your audience, create and efficiently run a page, advertise on the platform, and even make money on it.

Creating the perfect Facebook page can take your business to new heights. If you want to market your product successfully, you have to exploit the potential of Facebook to the fullest.

So, what are you waiting for? Without any further ado, let's get started and learn everything there is to know about Facebook as a branding tool.

Chapter One: The Early Stages

In this chapter, we will be focusing on the following three steps – researching audience demographics, finding out their key areas of interest and learning to use Facebook audience insight.

Step 1: Discovering your Facebook Audience

Some beginners believe that you should establish an identity before knowing your audience. In most cases, however, it's the opposite. Before you start posting and decide what you want, it's important to first know what your audience wants to see. Different products and services from different niches cater to unique consumer personas - an abstract collection of concepts and characteristics that businesses attribute to their target market to meet their standards and preferences.

On Facebook, you may find more than a handful of different personas, so narrowing your business's target to just one or two can help make your efforts more fruitful.

Consider this, two businesses, Business 1 and Business 2 have both just started their Facebook pages to extend their reach and become visible to their market on the biggest online platform around.

Business 1 is a furniture retail store that offers low-priced pieces that are mainly made from composite material. They're light, budget-friendly, and come in large quantities since they're mass-produced in the company's factories. While some products are available for purchase through their partner furniture stores in some malls, most of their items can be found through their website, which is the main focal point of their revenues.

Business 2 is a bespoke furniture manufacturer. They sell high-end solid wood pieces made from maple, New Zealand pine, and birch wood. Their pieces are heavy, one-of-a-kind, and unique, with only one piece available per design. They sell their items in a studio, which is the main center of their business. Facebook and all other online channels are simply for information dissemination - they share info on how to take care of solid wood, how to tell apart different kinds of wood, as well as share other relevant articles that are published on their official blog.

The truth is, both brands sell furniture. So, you could say that they're in the same niche, but do you think these two are competing? More importantly, do you think they should use the same strategies to appeal to their respective markets?

While both Business 1 and 2 operate in the furniture market, they've got two completely different goals. The first aims to provide its buyers with budget-friendly options that are easily accessible over the Internet and through several retail stores in malls in the area. The second one, on the other hand, leans more towards art and selling furniture, not for its inherent usefulness, but its beauty. So, the brand caters mostly to collectors and high-income individuals who have the luxury of paying for these types of items. It goes without saying that Business 1 and Business 2 are trying to appeal to completely different consumer personas.

Business 1 is looking for budget-conscious buyers who are looking for a quick purchase and are more interested in function than form. Business 2, on the other hand, is looking for buyers who are willing to spend more and are in search of aesthetically pleasing places rather than functional ones, and who are likely to go to the store to make a purchase.

Now that this idea has been established, both brands can now come up with an aesthetic and identity to make sure that they're appealing to their audience in the best possible way.

Step 2: Needs of the Audience

In the same light, it's important that you consider the specific needs, preferences, and thoughts of your buyers. In doing so, you won't waste your time and effort coming up with marketing material that will fly over their heads.

To get an idea of your Facebook consumers' persona, ask yourself the following questions:

What age are they?

Looking back at the example shared above, it's easy to assume that the first business would probably appeal to younger buyers - college students, small families, single professionals - those who are more interested in the function of the item rather than the way it looks. The second business would be better off aiming its marketing strategy at older individuals with the money to purchase such expensive pieces and those who see the inherent value of solid wood.

Knowing the average age of your consumer persona allows you

to communicate with them in terms of what they understand. Typically, younger generations respond to brands better when they adopt the current language, including meme culture and slang. For older individuals, sophisticated, professional tones of voice tend to communicate ideas more effectively.

What's the nature of their work?

You might think that your audience's employment shouldn't matter, but the significance of their work lies in the fact that it tells you more about their schedules. Facebook users who are office workers might be offline from 9 to 5, and online for the rest of the day as they commute home or relax in their own space. Retirees can be online any time of the day, so your peak hours for activity can be anywhere from the early hours of the morning until late in the evening, with a few dead spots in the middle as our seniors take their naps.

Consider the kind of products and services you're offering and try to figure out the specific work demographic that might be interested in them. For the most part, discovering your target market is a topic all on its own; however, there are online tools that you can use to help you learn more about the possible employment categories that might be most interested in what you offer.

How much do they make?

A large part of knowing how much your target market makes relies on knowing where they work. Understanding your buyer's budget is an essential aspect of marketing anywhere on the Internet. On Facebook, however, where almost everything is visual, knowing how much your buyers are willing to spend will help you format your pictures and other media to communicate the cost of your products and services.

For instance, recent surveys have found that brands that use fun, colorful images with lots of quirky graphics and playful fonts are typically characterized as budget-friendly. On the other hand, those that use dark images with fewer colors, dramatic imagery, and a sleek, sophisticated overall appeal are branded expensive and high-cost.

Why is this important? Knowing how much your target audience can spare for services or products like those that you offer can help you format your posts to meet their expectations. Tailoring your posts to communicate that your products and services are affordable to them will make it more likely for them to click through and learn more about your brand.

If, for example, a person who doesn't know your brand sees your post on their feed and finds that you sell something they want or need, then you might spark their interest.

However, once the initial discovery phase moves to the next phase of the consumer flowchart - which is determining cost - they might shy away from your brand if they cannot afford it. If you look too expensive, your budget-minded audience might feel like you're out of reach. If you look too affordable, on the other hand, those with more money to spend might question the quality of your products.

If you fail to communicate the right cost range with the way you market yourself on Facebook, you could lose valuable clicks that could bring potential consumers to your page.

What format of engagement works for them?

Not everyone wants to participate in polls, and not everyone wants to click through a link you provide to read a full-length article. So, to encourage engagement, think about your audience and what they'd like to see before you publish any content.

For instance, a page targeting mothers and grandmothers with family-related content might use heartfelt quotes pasted over visually stimulating images to tap into its readers' emotions. This content is likely to generate shares, tags, and comments, as their audience might feel a sense of familiarity or because the content might make them reminisce on days long gone.

This is completely different to a travel page that offers its reader's domain links that redirects to its website, where it shares information on the latest travel destinations and hotspots in the world. Why would its audience be willing to click through?

The answer is simple - because a traveling blog will provide a more accurate representation of the experience compared to a Facebook post. They're not likely to find that kind of content on the social media platform anyway since it is usually pretty long, so they'd be more than willing to read about it elsewhere.

Different formats work for different people with different interests – that's just the way social media works. Trying to put yourself in their shoes and listing the content that you like and are interested in and what you typically find to be a nuisance can help establish the best format for your brand.

Step 3: Facebook Audience Insights

Facebook Insights is a unique feature offered to all business pages which helps administrators determine the performance of their posts. It provides details on a variety of engagement aspects, and ultimately gives the marketer a clear understanding of which strategies work best with their intended audience.

To begin, go to your Facebook business page and click on Insight. The three sections that you now see tell you three important things about your page – the number of people who liked your page in the last week, people who saw your posts, and people who engaged with your content. Engagement refers to liking, sharing or commenting on what you've posted.

Actions on Page gives you the number of times the CTA was clicked on your page. This is the blue action button that you can find on the right side of your page, just beneath the cover photo.

Page Views provides information on how many times users visited your page on Facebook.

Page Previews are determined by counting the number of times people have hovered over your name or user image anywhere on Facebook to see your page preview.

If a user sees your ads or posts anywhere on their feed and it catches their attention, they can hover their cursor over your name or image and Facebook will present them a quick overview of your page. This preview will then determine whether or not the user finds it relevant or necessary to visit your page based on the limited information presented.

With Hoot Suite, it's hard to tell whether users would decide in favor of visiting their page. For starters, none of the recent images show any text that gives an idea as to what other products, services, and promotions the business offers. This is another reason why the factors of a good photo post (discussed in upcoming chapters) are something that Facebook marketers must be careful to observe.

Page likes are the number of new fans your page has gained over a specific period of time When available, Facebook will break down the numbers into paid and unpaid, showing you whether likes were generated by your paid advertisements or by your organic posts.

Reach is the number of times Facebook users saw your posts and ads throughout the platform. The number increases every time any of your posts appears on any user's screen. If the data is available, Facebook will present reach divided between organic posts and promotions.

Recommendations are a type of response that people can provide to their friends when they post on their profiles in search of reputable and reliable sources for certain goods and services. For instance, if a friend posts about looking for nearby Italian restaurants that serve a specific type of dish, his friends have the option to mention a page. If one of his friends knows your business as a possible recommendation, they can mention your page as a response to the inquiry. These are then tallied and presented to you in your metrics.

Another way that Facebook counts recommendations is through users' posts. When they check-in to a business, they have the option to recommend it. So, if for example, a user checks in to a local hotel and posts a photo with the hotel tagged as a location, they can leave a short note at the end of the post to tell their friends whether they recommend the place or not. It helps Facebook users get trusted input on establishments and businesses near them by finding out whether or not their friends enjoyed their products or services.

CHAPTER ONE: THE EARLY STAGES

Post engagements are made up of likes, comments, and shares generated by your posts and promotions. The tallied score shown in the Insights summary consists of all engagement produced across all of your posts. To see how each specific post performed, there's a separate section at the bottom of the page that breaks down engagement for each image, video, and other content on your page.

Video insights are unique as they measure the number of minutes of video users across the platform have watched. So, if you have a one-minute long video, and ten people watched it to its completion, you'll have a total of 10 minutes viewed in your metrics. If two extra people only watched the first ten seconds, then your total would be at 10 minutes and 20 seconds.

What's nice about this unique measurement system is that it tells you at what point viewers might choose to stop watching your video and scroll past it. For instance, if you notice that several initial viewers stopped watching a specific video post within the first 10 seconds, then you can deduce that something about the first few moments of that video is unappealing or uninteresting to most people who view it. This way, it becomes easier for marketers to figure out the best strategies to keep viewers hooked until the end of each video.

Page followers shows you how the number of likes on your page increases over time. The metrics can also show you where on Facebook your page was liked, such as on your page itself or on the feed. Getting a better idea of when your page experienced an increase in likes can help you determine what particular strategy was able to create more interest.

Finally, the Order section tells you how much your page has earned over a specific period. These numbers become available if you have a shop or offer option on your page that lets users purchase directly.

If you Scroll down a little further on the Insights tab, you will see another section that shows the performance of your page's most recent posts. This part of the Insights feature shows you the type of post, the audience you've set for it, its reach, and the engagement it has created since posting. Facebook also makes it easier to access the Boost function by placing it as an option alongside each post, so you can easily pay for increased attention for posts that perform better than others.

Choosing to Boost a Facebook post brings up a prompt that allows you to configure an ad out of the post you chose to boost. Much like other ads, these can contain a CTA button, a targeted audience, and a set budget depending on how much you're willing to spend. Typically, more advanced pages are urged to consider personalizing ads instead of using existing posts to Boost, since custom ads tend to work better. Nonetheless, the personalized ones are convenient and reasonable for smaller businesses.

At the bottom of the Insights tab, there is a section labeled Pages to Watch. Here, you can add pages that you consider your inspiration or your competition, and compare how your page performs compared to them. This feature is something most SMEs should be keen on using since it provides insight as to how other pages in the same niche perform using their strategies.

If you notice a sudden increase in their total engagement or page likes, you can check their page and see how they've changed their marketing strategy to appeal to their audience. If you closely watch the right competition in the same market that you're trying to target, you might be able to learn from their techniques and apply them to your own business.

Chapter Two: Branding

I n this chapter, we will focus on the next three steps that are an essential part of branding – creating a Facebook page, creating your brand identity and setting up an email option within your Facebook page.

Why is Facebook marketing important?

Facebook is the new way to market your products. If you correctly tap into the potential that Facebook has, you will be able to market your products successfully. Facebook marketing is based on trying to capture the imagination of your audience in new and interesting ways. If you can get your audience to relate to your products, then you'll be able to sell it to them.

If you have an established audience, then you can definitely use Facebook to influence people to create a positive attitude towards your products. A lot of companies use this strategy; they hire exceptional social media managers to help create a positive image for the product and increase its reach. You can do all of this by yourself, and all you have to do is understand how important Facebook is, set up your page correctly, and understand how advertising works.

Facebook is especially important for small businesses. These businesses do not have a lot of money that they can use to invest in expensive advertisement campaigns. However, they can use Facebook to create a fan following and increase awareness about their products and get to the level where they can afford expensive advertisement campaigns.

Number of Users

Facebook is the biggest social media platform available to any marketer. It has over four hundred million active users, with people who actively use their accounts on a daily basis. If you advertise correctly, then you can reach out to a lot of these people and make them aware of your product.

Customer Interaction

Customer Interaction is extremely important as it creates customer loyalty. A customer always prefers a business that adds a personal touch. The reason for this is pretty simple - every customer wants what is best for him. The business that treats him better and with more kindness is the one that they would naturally gravitate towards. On Facebook, through posts and comments, you can connect directly with your customers. In real life, connecting with each person directly is impossible. That is why Facebook is extremely useful as you can reply to each comment and take all of their queries, which shows to your customer that you care about them and their needs.

It allows you to attract more customers, as a customer will always prefer a business that gives a personal touch to whatever they are doing. The reason behind this is that the customer feels like the business cares about him. Many big companies can't connect with every one of their customers directly and these customers feel like they are not being heard and not being taken care of. Therefore, it's important for them to feel like they matter to your business, and Facebook is the perfect way to do this.

Search Engine Optimization

SEO is important for any business, as it's a way to get your business popular on Google. If you have a Facebook page, it will show up first when someone Googles the name of your business. If you do not have a Facebook page, then it might be difficult for someone to find information about your business. Whenever you Google something, Facebook links appear at the top, and that's why they are significant.

Free Promotion

Facebook equals free promotion. If people like your page, your content shows up on their news feed. If they comment on your post or share your status, then it further promotes other people to like your page, and they get to know more about your business. This is a free method of promotion, and you don't have to do anything at all. This might not be very effective, and it might take a lot of time to build a huge fan following, but even if it helps you get a couple of loyal customers, then that's already good, as you didn't have to spend any money, yet still got a few new customers.

Also, your page could go viral. If your posts are interesting and you use interactive material like memes, puns, etc. to promote your page, you could gain people's interest. They will share stuff like this, and this will garner you an even a bigger fan following. Free promotion is extremely important for any small business, and if you work hard for it, you can benefit.

Responding to Problems

If you are on Facebook, you can quickly respond to any issues that may arise. If there is an issue, then you can make a post about it and inform your customers, and this helps you to tackle problems efficiently. It further helps you to respond to customers' problems because they can message you on the platform, and you can quickly attempt to solve their issue. It's difficult for a business to be available all the time, but when you're on Facebook, you are always available. Even if you can't solve the problem at the exact moment, the customer can still directly connect with you and thus feels like their voice was heard.

Beating your Competition

The best way to get an edge over your competition is with the help of Facebook. It's a competitive market out there, and everyone is trying to do better than their competition, so Facebook might be the edge that you need to beat it.

If your competition is on Facebook and you aren't, you are already two steps behind. Facebook can be the difference between you and your competition, which is why it is so important.

There is a lot of competition in the food industry, and almost every restaurant out there has a Facebook page. People even decide where they want to go on the basis of the reviews that they see on the Facebook page of a restaurant. This can be the deciding factor for a customer who is confused between you and your competition, so you have to make sure that you capitalize on this opportunity by having a Facebook presence and by keeping your page active.

Customized News Feed

People won't see your posts on their news feed just because they have liked your page, as Facebook has various ways to determine what posts appear. More than anything else, the factor that determines a post on someone's news feed is that person's interest. If a person has an interest in a particular thing, then all related things will show up on their news feed first.

So, if a person is a huge fan of food and has liked a lot of Facebook pages related to food, they will see posts by restaurants they have liked on their news feed.

You can use this to your advantage by posting content that matches the interests of a person. If a person has liked your page, then they have an interest in your business. So, try to post content that is related to your business but at the same time is interesting enough to hold a person's attention.

This gives you a great opportunity to get into people's news feeds. You can use this Facebook algorithm to make your page even more famous by posting relevant and interesting content.

Facebook also shows things that are more famous first, so the posts that match your interests and that your friends have liked are shown first. This is why posting engaging content is very important; the more likes and shares you get, the better the chances are of a person seeing your posts in their news feed. You should try out your posts on a specific group of people to see how engaging it is as this will help in ensuring the long-term viability of your Facebook page.

You have to work on your Facebook analytics; try to see what kind of content your audience is interested in and work on your future content based on this data. Always remember who your target audience is so that you can customize your content according to them.

Social Reputation

Social reputation is not about how many likes you have or how active your user base is, but simply about having a presence on social media. The businesses that are not on Facebook are at an inherent loss because they will never be able to market their products or services as well as their competitors.

Social reputation is simply about having a page; if you don't have a Facebook page, then you will never have a social reputation. Now, the consequences of not having a social reputation stem from user behavior. A consumer will always prefer businesses that he believes are legitimate and who work hard to gain customers. You can gain this legitimacy by being on Facebook, as many users nowadays tend to search the name of a business on Facebook to determine if they want to become customers.

If you are not on Facebook, then there is a sizeable amount of people that may not even take your business seriously, and therefore, you'll never become a reputed seller to them.

Step 4: Facebook Page

Facebook bases all its interactions on two things – profiles and pages. A profile introduces a person, whereas a page introduces a company or business. A profile is created for an individual looking to represent themselves on Facebook, whereas a page is created by an individual to represent their company or business. The same individual can create an individual profile for himself as well as a page for his or her company.

On a profile, you can add friends, as others using Facebook will appear in the list of friends. These can be friends, family members, and acquaintances. A page, on the other hand, can have likes and followers. Likes refer to the number of people who like the particular page, and in turn, the company in question. These can be known or unknown people as it is impossible to know who has liked a page.

A profile's activity generally shows up in the news feed rather than a page's feed. A person has to visit a page to know what is happening on its feed.

There is also the option to create a group on Facebook. A group is a place where like-minded people can join and collaborate. A person can create a group and invite others to join in, and it can be a closed or a public group depending on the creator's preference. However, it is impossible for a business to own a group, so it is important to create a page for it. However, a business profile can still partake in a group if necessary. We will discuss groups in further detail later on in this book.

Setting up a Facebook Page

The very first step is to create a page. To do this, log onto Facebook.com, and click on the 'create a page' button at the bottom of the page. This is easy if you already have a Facebook account as you can easily create a page by signing into your existing account. Alternatively, you can go to Facebook.com/pages and create a page. Then, you have to understand the different terms and conditions.

Once you have done that, you can enter the name of the page. Remember to take your time and not to rush this decision. It is best to consult with friends and family before coming up with a name for the page. Once the page has been created, Facebook allows just one change of name.

Once done, you can click on the type of business that you own. You will have to choose one from the following options:

· Local business or place
· Company, Organization or Institution
· Brand or Product
· Artist, Band or Public Figure
· Entertainment (promotion)
· Cause or Community

Once you choose the appropriate option, you can move on to the next step of the process. Next, you can fill in the 'About' section before adding your website's address. Once done, Facebook will give you the unique URL for your page.

Next, you can choose the preferred page audience; if you have content for people above 18 years of age, you have to specify it to your audience. If you are not ready with your page yet, go to the settings, edit the page visibility and choose "un-publish page" to continue editing the page without being disturbed.

After putting in the requested information, Facebook asks for additional details. Later on, this information will be displayed on the published page to help viewers get in touch with you more easily. If you don't want users to locate you using your exact address (which is the case for most home-based businesses), you can tick the box at the bottom to hide the exact information and provide just the area instead.

Why is it important to add your area or address? While most

small-sized enterprises operating from a home address want to keep that information private, it's important to keep in mind that Facebook uses location as the main factor to provide its users with relevant search results. For instance, a person in California in search of a landscaping service would likely find Facebook inefficient at finding what they need if it were to show businesses from Maine or Oregon.

The following are the different page elements you can choose while setting up:

Page visibility – here, you can choose who can view your page. If you want to make it a private page, you can modify the settings and make it a closed group.

Posting visibility – here, you can choose who can post on your page. Sometimes, it's important to limit them so that you don't end up with a page with a million posts.

Targeting and privacy for posts - this is to capture a particular audience. It is important to target the posts to a certain audience, in order to send the message across to the right people.

Messages – this refers to the messages that your page can receive. If you are taking orders from people through your Facebook profile, then you can create filters to keep spam at bay.

Tagging ability - people who can tag your page.

Country restrictions - people from specific countries that can view your page. Sometimes, it's best to limit the page only to countries where your business operates so that you don't receive spam.

Age restrictions - people of specific age groups can view your page.

Page moderation - this allows you to prevent certain words from appearing on your page to avoid spamming.

Profanity filter - this is to prevent people from using profanity.

Delete a page - If you don't like it, you can delete a page and start from scratch.

Category - pick a category for your company - this is quite important, as it will make it easier to find you.

- Name - the name of your company
- Start information - you can mention the details of when your company started
- Short description - you can provide a short description of your company
- Long description - a detailed description of what your company is all about
- Company overview - you can provide an overview of your company
- Mission - you can mention your company's mission
- When founded - the date when your company was founded
- Awards - any awards that your company may have won
- Phone number - your company's phone number
- Website - your company's website

Once you fill in the above details, your page will be ready to roll.

Here is a look at the Facebook page standards:

Profile Picture

After filling in the information, the first thing Facebook asks users to do is to add pictures, which includes the profile image and the cover photo that works as a banner. Uploading these photos helps give your brand an identity. As your business grows, these initial photos can make it easier for buyers to recognize you in a sea of companies that might offer the same products and services

According to research, businesses with clearly defined profile pictures tend to perform better than those with poor image choices. Despite that, business profiles with a picture regardless of whether or not it meets consumer standards will generally perform better than business pages that don't have a user image at all.

When choosing a user image, it's a lot easier to make the wrong choice than to make the right selection on the first try. This is especially true if you're a small start-up that doesn't necessarily have a brand logo yet. If you're not quite sure what image to use as your profile picture, consider these pointers:

Know the Guidelines

To ensure uniformity across its platform, Facebook enacts a few guidelines that direct marketers towards making the right choices, to help make sure that their brand is recognized even through a small user image, no matter where it pops up on the platform.

The first thing you need to know about user images is that first, it needs to be square. Across Facebook, the places where your profile picture might appear are either round or square shaped, but they retain essentially the same proportions. This means that if your image is cut into a circle shape, such as throughout the comments, your image should still be recognizable to your audience.

Also, according to Facebook, your user image can't be any smaller than 180 x 180 PX. This is to ensure image quality, as anything smaller might end up looking pixelated on your page. Finally, Facebook discourages the use of text on profile pictures for business pages. These tend to complicate the look of your icon and make it difficult for your audience to appreciate what you're trying to show them, especially if the user image is presented in its smallest form.

Less is More

Many SMEs tend to think that packing a small image with more information works better to communicate who they are and what they offer, but the truth is, it is actually the opposite. Uploading a profile picture that uses less color, text, and images or graphics can help establish a brand. That's because these uncomplicated images are easy to pick out in a crowd and it eliminates the need for users to have to squint to make sense of your image.

For instance, consider Nike and Adidas - two of the most prominent sporting brands. Sure, their logos change colors every now and then, and Adidas has a few variations to its existing logo, but one thing remains true for both companies - there isn't a lot going on with their logos, but it works, because it's simple, easy to digest, and highly recognizable. Even when presented as a tiny 43 x 43-pixel icon next to a comment on Facebook, you'd be able to tell what brand it represents.

Prevent Change

If and when you decide to change your user image, it's like a total rebrand. So, ensure that you're ready for a potential dip in popularity. The fact is, using the same user image over a long period helps make it easier for prospects and buyers to recognize you, so maintaining it guarantees that they'll know who you are at a glance.

If you suddenly decide to change your user image and then publish a post, your updated profile picture might confuse some of your audience - even the oldest fans you may have. They may think - who is this page and why is it showing up on my feed?

Unless they have the time to perform due diligence to find out who you are, they might hover over your name and unlike the page - just like that. Unless you're confident that you can pull off a successful rebranding effort, like Airbnb for example, then it would be in your best interest to stick to the first user image you've chosen. If you can't resist the urge to replace it, consider adding a relevant seasonal change instead of replacing it altogether.

For instance, Coca-Cola uses the Santa hat graphic on top of its logo to help add a festive touch to its page. The brand has been so successful at maintaining the same practice throughout the years that they've become something of an iconic holiday staple, and their Christmas logo is now an iconic image all on its own.

The cover photo, on the other hand, isn't quite as essential as the profile photo, but it does help give visitors a better idea of what you offer. Think of the cover photo as your digital storefront - if it's enticing enough, you might be able to get potential consumers to scan through your items and services. If it's cluttered, confusing, or irrelevant, they might shy away from your brand at a glance.

Here are the specifications for the profile picture,
- The picture must be square
- It must be at least 180x180 pixels
- It should display at 160x160 pixels on a computer

- It should display at 140x140 pixels on smartphones
- It should be 50x50 pixels on feature phones
- You must leave a space around, so the picture does not go all the way to the edge
- It is best for companies and businesses to use the company logo

Cover photo

Unlike your profile picture, the cover photo can be changed regularly. Much like a physical storefront, this is where businesses can showcase their latest offers and promotions to help keep their prospects and buyers updated. The position of the cover photo on your page also makes it exceptionally effective as a promotional banner, giving your visitors a clear, concise summary of what your page is all about.

Aside from that, the cover photo can also drive traffic to your page. How? When a user hovers over your icon, they're greeted with a page preview that's almost like a miniature version of your page. The preview contains a slightly larger user image, a copy of the cover photo, your page category, number of likes, a short description, and the last 3 images that you've published.

Along the bottom of the preview, there are a few action buttons that users can choose to contact you or interact with you directly without having to visit your page. The function of the cover photo shifts from digital storefront to potential hook.

Uploading a cover photo that uses a clear image describing your current focus in a large, minimal text can entice consumers to click through and visit your page. For instance, consider how AT& T did it in June of last year.

Albeit slightly darkened out by the standard overlay that

Facebook uses for its previews, it's easy to see that the AT&T page was emphasizing on Pride month. The update was posted in June, which was designated as the official month of celebration and awareness for the LGBT community. By updating their cover photo when these communities come together to commemorate their journey as a unique group, AT&T effectively showed support to all those involved.

You can assign a variety of functions to your cover photo. It all depends on your preference and how far your creativity will take you, but to guide you with your decision, try to keep these cover photo aspects in mind:

· It can be seen as a preview when users hover over your profile photo anywhere on Facebook

· Its strategic location on your page makes it one of the first things that your visitors will see

· Its rectangular format means it's best to design it in the form of a banner

· It doesn't dictate your identity like your user photo does, but creating its design and aesthetic based on your brand identity will make for a more cohesive page.

For the cover picture:

· It is recommended to use an 851x315 pixels, RGB, JPG picture that is less than 100 kb

· You can use the graph provided by Facebook to crop the image to the right size. It is best to use a picture that is easy on the eyes and not too overwhelming.

Calls to Actions

Remember that it is extremely important for you to guide your audience and tell them what to do on your page. Many people assume that people understand whatever they are supposed to do on a page; however, it pays to give them clear instructions.

It is best to create a "call to action" button that will allow your audience to take appropriate action. You must also clearly mention it in words to drive the message across.

Facebook Posts

Here are the specifications for Facebook posts:

The news feed images should be 472x394 pixels and have an actual ratio of 236x197 pixels, and the image should be 504x504. If you need help with this specification, you can use tools such as Picmonkey.com and Canva.com.

Posting to page

· Post links – you can post unique links to your page by adding them to the page

· You can pick a picture of your choice and then post it on the page

· You can also schedule your posts and post them at regular intervals

· You can edit the picture by hitting the edit button; you will have a glimpse of how others are seeing it

· If you do edit it, you can copy the new link and paste it in the box

· It is best to check all your work before posting it as you can avoid later having to delete it

· It is quite convenient to post multiple pictures at once

- You can also add a short description to each post
- You can easily tag people in your pictures
- You can use the # to look for someone who has been tagged
- You can also tag posts the same way and look for them using the #

Additional things to do on Pages

- When you upload a picture or a video, you have the option to add your location, but be cautious and only post location if necessary
- The video you wish to upload should be of a certain size. You can check the limitation of the video before uploading it
- You will be notified once your photos and videos have been uploaded
- Remember, videos will not automatically upload the audio, and you must add it separately
- For the event milestones tab, you can check the drop down options and choose the options that suit your requirements
- You can use the milestones option to have a better idea of the company, its various posts and the different people who can post on it
- You can control the various tabs by clicking the "manage tabs" option and edit it to your liking.
- One important point to note while posting on a company page is to log out as the admin and log into your profile before commenting, but if you have hired someone to manage the page, then they can be instructed to reply through the account or create another one.
- It is extremely important to share your business page on your personal timeline as it helps with capturing a bigger audience. After all, the main motive behind creating a page is to gather as big a crowd as possible, so it is important to advertise it

extensively in order to be noticed by as many people as possible.

· Remember that your page is synonymous with your company, and vice versa. You have to maintain a professional tone while posting on the page and instruct the person managing the page to do so too.

Do You Need a Page Manager?

If you research the Internet for ways to more easily manage your Facebook page, you'll find many applications and online software choices that promise to reshape your page to make it simpler, more straightforward, and more convenient. If you're thinking of diving into this and paying the purchase costs or membership fees, consider the following points:

Facebook might not be your main social media platform. Let's throw that out there. Yes, Facebook is a very large and promising platform, and for beginners, it can be a great start, but just because of the opportunities that the platform presents, it doesn't mean it will be your main social media platform for the rest of your business's life. There are many great platforms out there that can provide a function that's more attuned to your needs and preferences, so you might find yourself switching your main social media efforts to a different platform.

There's nothing wrong with that. There are tons of brands that prefer Instagram to Facebook because it's easier to achieve an aesthetic and to reach your audience with hashtags. If you're just starting out and are not a hundred percent sure that Facebook is the best primary social media platform for you, consider first learning more about it before you invest in paid apps or onboarding a new team member.

If you take a peek at the insights tab of your page, you'll find that the metrics contain all the basic information you need to be able to understand your target market at the beginner level. It's complete, concise, and easy to understand, so any applications that don't expound these numbers might not offer you much else. Those that do have a lot more information might be overwhelming for a beginner and may make managing your page confusing and daunting. Try to keep it as simple as you can to try to learn the ropes.

It's low cost. Unless you have the budget to shell out as you first create your SME, you might be more interested in saving than spending everything you've got on your digital marketing strategy. There are many great brands out there that became big corporations without having to shell out millions at the start, and you can achieve something to the same effect.

Facebook offers all its tools for free; only the ads require payment. This helps keep your small business's budget intact so that you can get all the information you need to make intuitive choices without having to spend on something that Facebook can already do.

Is there ever a right time to get a social media marketer onboard or buy an expensive Facebook page management software? The answer is yes - there's a time for everything, as long as it's the practical and intelligent choice for your brand.

If the time comes that you feel you need to relieve yourself of non-core functions like social media management, you might want to utilize something that eases the process, but if you're only starting and you have the time to work on your page and social profiles, then anything you spend to make it "easier" might very well, in fact, be an unnecessary expense.

Brand Identity

Now that you've got the basics of your page all set up, your next task is to make it functional and appealing to your consumers. During this second step, it's important to keep one key factor in mind - most Facebook users don't completely read information that's laid out in front of them.

In a recent survey, it was discovered that Facebook users tend to skim through chunks of text in search of something relevant. If a text is too long and drawn out, they won't bother with it and might skip it entirely.

Therefore, creating a brand identity is all about taking your page and design it in a way that is memorable for the audience.

Writing a Page Description

As you explore the different areas and sections of your new Facebook page, you'll find that some parts require you to fill out information. For instance, as the platform presents your initial page, one of the primary tasks it will ask you to complete is to "Add a Short Description." This snippet of information is something like a business bio - a quick summary of who you are and what you offer.

When writing your page description, there are a few good practices you might want to keep in mind:

· Add a touch of SEO. What are you offering? Keep in mind that Facebook pages get indexed in Google search engine results if it's relevant to the user's search. For instance, typing something like "catering services" on Google returns with a specific Facebook page as the top result after paid ad placements. So, slipping in the generic product name or service type into your description could bump up your chances of popping up on Google.

· Avoid technical jargon. Big, confusing words that only mean something to a select few can be hard for the average Joe to appreciate. If you're running a diagnostics clinic, for example, using medical terminology that's exclusive to your industry might not translate well in terms of end-user comprehension. Just keep it simple and avoid big words that might not be readily understood by the majority.

· Redirect your readers. If you impress your viewers with your description, they might want to see what you offer right there and then. Adding a link that leads to your official website will help make it easier and convenient for them to learn more about you. If they have to navigate to your page or search Google to find your business website, they might give up before finding it.

Setting Your Action Button

There's a single, bright blue button on your page that viewers can use to take action. This is the single most powerful tool on your entire page because it encourages readers to engage with your business. By properly programming your action button, you can make it easier for viewers to reach you or even start their purchase.

When you click the "+ Add a Button" option, you're provided with several choices that you can set as the main action that viewers can perform on your page. Each one serves a unique purpose, and some of them might be better suited to your business depending on the service or product you offer.

Book with You - This option sets the button to say, "Book Now." It's ideal for businesses like equipment rentals, hotels, and manual services like household cleaning, car washes, and so on. The Book Now button will redirect users to one of many different booking channels. Currently, Facebook offers "Appointments on Facebook" - a website feature that allows users to book appointments with businesses and receives updates and reminders on the app.

Some of the other booking channels that pages can use include Google Calendar, Booker, Booking Bug, Setster, SimplyBook.me, or an outbound link that leads to your unique booking website. If you have a booking tool that isn't on the list, you can request Facebook to add it to your page qualify it for your page.

Contact You - This is the most commonly used action button among all the available options, and it allows viewers to get in touch with businesses through a variety of channels. There are a few choices available for businesses depending on their preferred method of communication.

Both the Contact Us and Sign Up choices will redirect users to your official website where they can contact you, depending on the avenues you make available for them there. Send Message allows users to leave a message for you on Facebook which will be sent to your Messenger inbox. Call Now makes it easier for prospects to reach you by phone.

When clicked on a mobile device, it automatically dials an outgoing call using the number you provided in your information page. Finally, Send Email allows them to write a message to the email that you choose to indicate in the next step.

Learn More About Your Business - For businesses that offer revolutionary technology, a common question that Facebook visitors might ask is, "How does it work?" For instance, a new anti-aging product promises to remove the signs of aging in a matter of seconds using a special cream and a unique skincare 'wand' that uses a powerful laser to 'zap' away wrinkles. Sounds futuristic, doesn't it?

On its Facebook Page, a button that says "Learn More" encourages viewers to explore their tech, giving the business a better opportunity to explain how their product works. Alternatively, the "Watch Video" option can instantly pull up an instructional or informational video that can make the specifics of their tech more clear to consumers.

Shop with You or Make a Donation - Under this specific choice, Facebook Pages can either ask their visitors to "Shop Now" or "See Offers." Depending on which one you set, your viewers can be redirected to your Shop section, your Offers section, or your website.

Download Your App or Play Your Game - This button proves to be the most effective for app and game developers. Clicking on it will either redirect the user to the page owner's website, or even to the Play Store or the App Store depending on the device that they're using.

When choosing the right button for your page, it's important to keep the nature of your business in mind. For instance, using the "Book Now" button for a clothing retail brand wouldn't make sense, since there is nothing for consumers to book in the first place.

Another thing to consider is what's most convenient for you. For instance, if you choose to set the button as "Call Now" but find it taxing to have to keep answering phone calls, then perhaps you'd be better off choosing a different contact alternative.

After that's all set up, your page is pretty much ready to go. These basics should help you get started on your Facebook marketing strategy and should provide you with all the essentials you need to reap the benefits that the social media platform has to offer.

Branding Essentials

When it comes to setting up a killer page on Facebook, it is important to make it as interesting for your audience as possible. You must put in the effort to make it look as professional as possible to help your audience better connect with it.

Here are some Facebook page strategies that you can employ to make it entertaining for your audience:

<u>Personality</u>

It is important to add in a certain personality to your Facebook page. People should be drawn to it and feel the urge to like or comment on the page. If you settle for something mediocre, it will simply not work. A good idea is to hire professionals who are good at molding pages and making them interesting for the audience. You have to instruct them to review the audience and prepare an analysis of their general characters. Doing so helps in preparing a fitting schedule that will make your page popular. You can also look at the strategies that some of the other companies employ and come up with a similar plan; however, it is best to maintain a little originality and remain true to your company's policies.

It pays to have a good sense of who you are and what your company stands for. If you are confused about this, it will go against you. It is best to work out an image that you would like to portray and then keep it consistent. It's important to remember that things can look like one thing in your mind and another thing on paper. So, it is best to create a page and check to see if it looks like you envisioned it to be. check if it looks exactly like you planned it.

Consistency

Remember that consistency is key - You have to be both consistent and coherent with your posts. Your Facebook page should be a slice of your store and the products you sell. Don't make it too different as it can confuse your customers. If you have a team working for you, then instruct them to post at regular intervals, without keeping the audience waiting. A good trick is to know when people prefer to have an update come their way, and not make it boring, as you have to keep your audience engaged. Again, you can look at a successful company's strategy and come up with a posting schedule that suits your own. As mentioned earlier, it is best to aim for the early evening slot, as that's when most people are active on social media.

Frequency

When it comes to maintaining an online profile for your company, it is extremely important to post as frequently as possible. You must try to add new posts at regular intervals so that people know what to expect and when to expect it. A golden rule is to post in the evenings, as that is when most people expect new posts. Try to increase the frequency of the posts as the company grows. Some companies prefer to add new posts three times a day as that helps to keep the audiences glued, but it is important not to get carried away and post too many things at once. You should not overload the audience with too much information, as it will only end up confusing them, so keep the information relevant and coherent. You can always do a short trial and error to see what is working for you and what isn't. For example, you can ask your audience how often they would like to receive an email from you. If they are happy with the frequency, then you can keep it the same or change it according to their preferences.

Business Goals

It is important to be in sync with your business goals and update your page from time to time by keeping in mind the main goals. Your page should be a thorough representation of your company's motives and should speak of your ambitions. It should portray your true intentions. Also, it helps to incorporate some of your company's policies in every new post.

Converting your Profile to a Business Page

If you already have a Facebook profile and wish to convert it into a page without creating a separate one, you can do so with ease. Here is how:

Go to Facebookpage.com, and search for convert my Facebook page. There, you will be able to automatically convert your current profile into a page.

Click settings and download a copy of your Facebook page. Pick the profile to page migration option. Remember; once it is merged, you won't be able to retrieve your profile. You have to make up your mind before making the transition. To merge your business page, go to settings, choose the general tab and choose between the merge pages and merge duplicate pages and choose pages that you want to merge, but remember, the two pages have to be identical; including the same address and information, as otherwise, they will not merge into one.

It is easier to start from scratch and create a page dedicated to your company; however, you will have to fill in all the details from scratch.

"Page-only" Strategies

When it comes to promoting your Facebook page and using it the right way, it is best to adopt "page-only" strategies to enhance its appeal. This means that you run exclusive offers on your Facebook page, without having them anywhere else.

The following are some Facebook only strategies that you can employ.

Merchandise

It is a good idea to start with merchandise, which includes offering exclusive goods that are not available at the store. For example, you can offer a product that people can only buy through your Facebook page or website and not at the store. Alternatively, you can offer a customized product that is only available online, like offering to customize a product to the customer's liking by changing the color scheme or encrypting a message, for example. You can also offer a product in a color scheme or pattern that is different from whatever is available in store. You have to make it obvious that it is an online exclusive by making appropriate announcements. You can also tell people at your store to check it out online to divert their attention to your "page."

Offers

You can run exclusive online offers, which can include schemes such as buy 1 get 1 free or a complimentary gift, for example. Such offers are sure to generate interest and enhance your page's value. Again, it is important to advertise it in order to ensure that people are made aware of the offer. You can send out emails and tell people about the offers you have carved out for your online audience. You can also advertise it in your store or hand out flyers to people so that they visit your Facebook page.

Rewards

You can reward people who bring in likes. This works well as people will be prompted to bring in more and more people to like your page. The reward needs to be appealing enough to capture your audience's interest. You can offer coupons, free merchandise or specially designed merchandise. All of these can be quite appealing and help lure in more people to your page. You can announce it on the page as well as on other social media accounts. You can also mention it on your website and inform people who visit your physical store.

Discount coupons

You can offer discount coupons your customers which will give them a discount on the products and services that you offer in your store, and these will be made available only on the Facebook page. Again, you must announce it on all your social media accounts such as Twitter and Instagram to ensure that people are informed.

Contests

Contests are a fun way to get people to visit your page, as it helps people get involved, and you can announce it on your Facebook page. The contest can be related to the products or the services that you offer; it can be something like adding a tagline, completing a phrase, or posting pictures of the products. You must also offer a prize that is exciting enough for people to want to partake in the contest. Setting a short deadline is a must, as it will allow you to increase your page views in a short period of time.

Events

You can also announce events on pages, where people meet up and get to know each other better over some food and drinks.

Such events will also help you know your audience better.

If done correctly, events can be of great help. All you have to do is create an interesting event, invite as many people as you can, and spread awareness with the help of your page. So, try to promote your business and product with the help of an event. The benefit that you get from this is that you don't have to spend a ton of money sponsoring events organized by other people. A good idea is to sponsor local events for better name recognition.

You can use Facebook to get name recognition without spending a lot of money organizing events. Events can become popular if publicized in the right way; first, identify the kind of event that your target audience would be interested in, then start inviting people and spreading the word about it.

Say you are a local bakery in your area who wants better name recognition. Start by thinking of a creative event that you can use to publicize your bakery while at the same time giving your customers a good time. Create a related event on Facebook and start inviting people that you know are in your area; to do so, use your contacts as well as your Facebook page. Use the event to promote your bakery and keep advertising your bakery so that your small business gets name recognition.

This is just the beginning; by spending a little more money, you can create events that will attract thousands of people. Start slowly with events that you don't have to invest a lot in, and once you see that the events are helping you in streamlining revenue, you can start expanding to bigger events to get even more name recognition.

These are just some of the different offers you can run online, and you can modify them to suit your company's policies.

Chapter Three: The Basics of an Effective Landing Page

In this section, we'll learn about making an effective landing and capture page and creating a relevant lead magnet product.

The next step is to create a special landing page that contains your offer and email capture opt-in forms. You can either employ the services of a web developer or use a landing page generator service, such as www.leadpages.com or www.instapage.com. For a monthly fee, these websites offer a user-friendly service with various templates, design examples, and tutorials that will help you put your landing page together. Your landing page should match your goal, which at this stage will be to promote your offer visually and to get the email addresses of potential customers.

The web pages that you are trying to redirect your visitors to are called 'landing pages'— the first web page a visitor lands in after clicking your ads and links. Any web page that you visit is considered a website landing page. Creating web-landing pages allows you to more efficiently convert a higher amount of guests into leads. The web landing pages make finding deals easier for your guests since they don't have to get around your website to find the site they're looking for. Directing your guests to web landing pages also eliminates any misunderstandings regarding what they must do to obtain your service, which keeps them from getting disappointed about not getting the right instructions, or determining that it's not worth their time. Therefore, guiding your guests to a web landing page, which is the actual web page with the offer the offer will make sure they turn into leads and the type they must finish to get it makes it more likely that they will finish your type and turn into leads.

Regardless of whether it's a paid search ad or an e-mail campaign that encourages someone to click an offer, the site where the individual ends up as he clicks has enormous potential to influence that individual into becoming a lead or customer. Web landing pages are a visitor's first impression of you and can create the difference between an 'okay' and a potential sale.

The web-landing page was particularly designed to help generate conversions. You want guests to turn into members, you want members to turn into leads, and you want leads to turn into clients. However, there are so many ways to build a web landing page, and it's hard to know which to use in advance, without the benefit of several weeks of examining with an A/B examining device tool, which design style and copy that will work better. Fortunately, a countless number of promoters and marketers before you have performed real campaign strategies and discovered through trial and analysis what performs and what doesn't.

The following are some fundamental things that you should consider when you design your landing page:

Keep It Simple:

One of the biggest conversion killers is misunderstanding. You don't want your web landing pages to look like your "designed by committee" business website. Your web landing pages need to be focused on conversion.

Get rid of sidebars, routing menu choices, needless design graphics, control buttons, and published text. Also, don't go insane on style design. This is business, not art. We're trying to generate a conversion, not win prizes.

Have a Unique Purpose:

Choices are great for economic potential, but they are bad for conversions on your web-landing page. The "Paradox of Choice" more often than not paralyzes our guests into not making any choice at all. Devote your landing page to one conversion objective. If you have another objective, create another landing page for that.

Keep your Promise:

Your web-landing page must meet the guarantee of the Search engines Ad, the e-mail topic subject line, the Twitter update, or the postcard you just sent by mail. Some of the biggest problems of Internet marketing promotion strategies have occurred when the guest clicks a web link because they were promised something in the title or headlines and discovered that the web-landing page had nothing to do with that headline.

Step 5: Lead Magnet

Just like what a magnet is used for, a lead magnet is a method used to attract leads to your business. In more sophisticated terms, a lead magnet it is a method or offer that is especially valuable to your prospective customers. They are willing to provide their contact information to receive something in return. One common misconception is that a lead magnet only works for online marketing, but it can also work for offline marketing too.

By including one at the start of your marketing campaigns, you will attract more targeted leads to your business. You will also reach that audience in a more effective way and on a more regular basis.

The best thing about a lead magnet is that you can keep it simple. You don't have to provide your audience with a 100-page report about your business or industry for it to work. Actually, it's important that the content isn't too extensive. That way, your audience will be more likely to read it. It's more important for your lead magnet to offer something of value than it is for it to be filled with lengthy content. If it isn't valuable, your audience won't want to download it. Then, your efforts would have been wasted.

Try building the content for your lead magnet around something you know your audience is struggling with. Think of a problem that keeps them up at night. This is where research plays a key role in developing a quality lead magnet as well as with helping you with your overall marketing campaign. Take the time to research your audience and learn as much as possible about them. Visit related social media platforms, forums, and your competitors to see what prospects are talking about, and how to meet their needs. Remember, the more people download or request your lead magnet, the more people enter your sales funnel. It also means they are more likely to come back to you for more.

Just as many types of businesses exist, there are also many types of lead magnets, and each one can be used effectively to reach a specific audience. Some common types of lead magnets include:

Book/ Guide/ Report:

A book, guide, or report is one of the most popular types of lead magnets. Generally, the content is based on your specific type of business or industry, and is geared toward helping your prospective customers solve a specific problem.

Another thing to remember with a book, report, or guide is that you don't have to be an online business to make it work. If you can show your prospects that your lead magnet offers them something valuable, you can send it to them by mail. Now that the novelty of email is starting to wear off, people look more forward to personalized communication through traditional mail. Sending them a real report or book in the mail gives them something tangible that can't just be filed away and forgotten like with an email.

Although you may have to spend a little more to make your book or report more visually and physically appealing, it may be worth it. You will also have to decide whether or not to charge a small shipping or handling fee to mail it out to recipients. By performing research on your competition and your market, you can determine what is commonly practiced in your industry and what your customers expect.

Tip Sheet/ Checklist/ Cheat Sheet Tip sheets or checklists are typically more suited for online businesses, though physical businesses shouldn't necessarily count them out. This type of lead magnet can revolve around your customer's need to follow a certain series of steps to accomplish a goal, and the checklist can provide a list of steps or resources the reader can refer to in specific circumstances. It can also share things to avoid or include when going through a specific process.

The key with this type of lead magnet is that your business must show how it can also assist in a specific situation. Whether the business needs additional help or assistance, your business should be featured as the place to go when they need a solution.

Free Class, Seminar or Training:

A free class or training session is usually best for businesses offering services. For example, if you provide financial services, you can offer a free class or seminar on managing finances or savings for retirement.

If you offer chiropractic services, you can provide two types of training, depending on your audience. You can either provide a free class to clients that revolves around how exercise and diet impact their overall health, which can be a great way to introduce yourself and your staff to prospective clients, but what if you sell information products to other chiropractors? You can then offer them free training that introduces them to those products.

One way that most businesses successfully implement a lead magnet of this type is to tell people what to do in the free training or seminar. Then, the next step would be to sell them with your services or products product on how to do it.

Survey or Quiz:

While this type of lead magnet isn't used as often, it still definitely should not be ignored. If you have an existing business, a survey can help you gauge and evaluate your customer's needs to make sure you're providing them with the types of products or services they're looking for. You can easily create a survey in a program like Survey Monkey that will integrate with your email so that you can track results.

If you're just starting, a quiz or assessment can also help to introduce your business. For example, if you provide website development services, you can use a free assessment on existing sites to get businesses to contact you for a consultation. This method can easily open doors to businesses by providing them with something valuable that can either save them money or help them increase sales.

Free Trial or Download:

Do you sell software or a group of information products to your clients? Or, do you offer a type of monthly service or subscription to them?

If so, a free trial or download could be the perfect way to introduce your business to prospective customers. Think of what some of the more popular subscription-based companies offer their consumers - companies like HBO and Amazon now offer 30-day free trials to get you to sign up and give out your contact and payment information.

If you don't have a service but have a book or information products, you can also offer the first few chapters of the book or the first product in a series for free to entice people to provide information to get that free download.

Chapter Four: Building an Audience

In this section, we will take a look at creating content to amass likes for your page, as well as how to work with ads.

Step 6: Posts

As you might have already noticed, there are a variety of posts that Facebook pages can publish to reach their audience with their message. The most common one you'll use - given the standards of a "quality" post - might be the photo post, so let's discuss that one first.

Photos

On average, Facebook users upload around 350 million photos a day. These range from personal images, to memes, announcements and news, and promotional business posts. As a brand page, you want to use photos more than any other type of post for two main reasons:

They generate more engagement

People feel more inclined to read, like, share, comment, or even save posts to their devices if they're visual. So, instead of posting plain text, you can try imposing your message over a relevant image to gain more attention and consumer engagement.

They're practical and easy

If visual posts are what works best, then shouldn't businesses be more inclined to publish videos than images? You'll notice that a lot of the popular pages on Facebook use videos more than any other post. While they can be just as (or even more) effective than photo posts, small businesses without marketing specialists might not be able to consistently create quality videos. Therefore, images tend to be the ideal post format for most small enterprises since virtually anyone can make them.

If you're trying to boost your business, what makes a good photo post? There are three main aspects that you should consider when coming up with concepts for your next big Facebook photo publication.

Copy

The first thing you need to start with is your copy. What do you want to tell your readers? While it is recommended that you keep the text on a photo to a minimum, you still need to add a few snippets of information here and there to get your marketing message across. Developing copy is a completely different story – and a long one, at that. For Facebook, however, all you need to keep in mind is that short, engaging snippets of text work best.

Aside from being short and succinct, Facebook copy works best when written in the form of a question. Copy that asks a simple "yes or no" question can get much more engagement than facts or opinions. Take this Walmart post, for example. During the heat of their summer campaign, the business's Facebook Page shared a few posts that got about 650% more engagement than anything else that they published.

The copy on the image itself was short and sweet – with two

large options that users could readily see even from the screen of a small handheld device. The choice was simple - like to vote for one item and share to vote for the other. It was easy, straightforward, and interesting for consumers, so thousands of people participated in the poll. Also, being able to slyly disguise engagement as a voting process made it possible for the post to spread far and wide. Re-engagement was also another witty aspect of the post, with some participants probably going back to the Walmart page to check the results of the poll.

In the caption copy, there's not a lot of information either, but it does give some details on their latest ice cream rollbacks. After quickly getting that info out of the way, the poll mechanics are reiterated in two lines, and the copy is complete. From a marketer's point of view, the campaign was short, sweet, and satisfyingly smart.

Imagery

Now that you've got a general message that you want to communicate to your audience, it's time to talk about the image itself. For small start-ups that don't have much money to spare for professional photographers and the like, there are royalty-free image hosting websites that house a plethora of stock pictures that can be used as your base for a photo post.

Keep in mind that since royalty-free images weren't specifically captured for your purpose, they might not be able to blend too well with your message or your brand. For instance, a business that operates in an African country might want to steer clear of stock images that depict Caucasian individuals, as their audience will not relate.

A good picture should be clean, bright, and minimalist. According to Facebook statistics, images with these qualities tend to work better for viewers because they don't require a lot of thinking or prolonged squinting to make sense of what's being presented to them.

So, what should your picture be? That all depends on you and your creativity. Think along the lines of visually attractive and interesting images that play with color, contrast, and perspective in order to create engagement and boost reach.

One Facebook business page we can all take cues from is Rihanna's Fenty Beauty. Offering products to a wide variety of skin tones, Rihanna's makeup brand boasts a collection that combines raw, earthy tones with electric pops of color, creating a beautiful contrast. The brand's Facebook photo posts are gloriously attractive, exuding an aesthetic that rings exceptionally well with its consumer base.

Size

Yes, image size matters. According to Facebook statistics, more than 80% of Facebook users access their profiles exclusively through a mobile phone. This - plus the fact that Facebook has quite a few image size restrictions on its platform - makes it imperative for marketers to pay close attention to the sizes of the photos they publish.

As a general rule, square images work best for users across all devices, because vertical rectangular screens can accommodate the square image in its entirety, and can contain the copy for that image on the screen at the same time. This gives your consumers a visual that properly communicates the message you're trying to convey.

When it comes to size, another thing you might want to consider is that low-resolution images will become pixelated and blurry after being uploaded to Facebook. Unfortunately, that's just one of the downsides of the platform, since they're not able to retain the sharpness of the original images. Opting for a high-resolution image that pushes the bounds of the image size that Facebook allows can ensure that you have images of good quality.

Step 7: Paid Photo Ads

Paid ads increase your reach and allow you to appear on the News Feed of Facebook users that might not have been easy to reach organically. Ad placement gets you more engagement; it opens the potential for more likes, and of course, helps drive sales. A great example of a success story using paid ads on Facebook is the one of World Weekly News - a page that managed to go from 3,000 something to 4,000 Facebook fans in just four days thanks to their effective paid ad strategy.

At the time, Facebook had limitations on the types of photo ads they allowed pages to submit to their paid ad feature. Back then, Facebook would only accept ads and publish them if they contained 20% text. This means that only 20% of the entire photo could be made up of text, while the other 80% had to purely be image. These days, Facebook has removed that limitation, though they do give this warning: the more text your image contains, the shorter its reach.

Since changing its standards, Facebook has also removed the special grid that measures text-to-photo ratio. Instead, it now uses a classifying system that tells you how much text your image contains before you publish it. Based on its standards, Facebook can classify your image as OK, low, medium, or high.

As a Facebook business marketer, your goal should be to aim for the OK category, since this is what Facebook considers ideal. The closer you land to OK, the more likely Facebook will favour your ad and bump it up as a priority post. As you get closer to the High category, the platform might choose to show your ad less, since those with lots of text perform less effectively.

Why does Facebook do this? It all works in favor of Facebook users. Statistics have shown that users tend to see lengthy texts as tedious and often not worth their time, especially if it's trying to sell them something. If Facebook insists on pushing these text-riddled photos on more feeds, they risk damaging the satisfaction of their users. So, they curtail the ads and give priority to those that might leave a more positive impression on their users.

Now, the tricky part - how do you decide how much you should pay for your ads? There is no magic number, and you'll have to decide this based on your budget, your needs, and the size of your business.

An essential factor that Facebook marketers need to understand is that the amount you pay isn't exchanged for ad space. You're not buying placement - you're bidding for it. With billions of users on the platform and millions of businesses that pay for ads, it's impossible for Facebook to provide a space for every one of the brands that pay for placement. Users aren't on Facebook for the ads anyway, and flooding the platform with too much copy and sales talk could negatively impact the platform's traffic.

So, paying for your ads doesn't always mean that you'll get as much exposure as the next guy, but it does give you the chance to reach a wider audience. Now, the priority that Facebook will give your bid depends on your engagement, size, and the number of clicks you generate on the platform. The higher your metrics, the more likely Facebook will bump you up their list of prioritized placements.

Consider this scenario, Business XYZ with a Facebook Page

with 500 likes spent $80 for ad placements. The promotion was set to last four days, with a budget of $20 per day. At the end of the promotion period, the page gained 50 new likes, 3,500 post engagements, and increased sales by 10% - which is not bad at all.

Happy with the sudden improvements they experienced throughout the duration of the ads, the brand bumped up their budget to twice the amount for the same length of time. At the end of the promotion, they earned another 50 new likes, 4,000 post engagements, and a 9% sales increase. Was it worth it?

At some point in your business's development, a bigger budget won't necessarily mean greater returns. Your reach can only do so much, and even if you widen it beyond what you'd be able to do organically, you might not be able to generate the positive results that you expect. This can be attributed to the fact that at the end of the day, Facebook gets to choose who it shows on their placements.

The reason why Business XYZ's increased ad payment strategy didn't provide proportionally larger returns is that it didn't change metrics over the span of 4 days. Essentially, all the features that Facebook uses to decide how often to show their ads didn't improve dramatically enough to prioritize the post.

So, even if you try to spend more in the hope of extending your reach, if your metrics don't qualify, Facebook might not allow it. Now, back to the initial question - how can you decide on the right budget for your paid ads? Simple - start small, and work upwards from there. After your first round of paid promotions, consider bumping up your daily budget by around $ 15 - $20.

If engagement and reach continue to increase proportionally, consider increasing your budget again. Once it plateaus, you can cap it off for the meantime until you start to see any dramatic changes to your metrics. When you do, bump your budget up again and see how it affects your page's performance.

Videos

Now that we've got one of the most basic Facebook post formats covered, it's time to move on to a common favorite among some of the most prominent brands on the platform. The video post format is fun, interactive, and highly informative, allowing marketers to share more information in bite-sized, easy to digest pieces with captions that shift as the video progresses.

Generally, small business owners try not to tread into video publishing territory because it's seen as a more professional skill. While it does share quite a few qualities with photo posts, videos come with their own unique guidelines that make them slightly trickier for page administrators to perfect.

Since we discussed the qualities of a good photo post, it's only appropriate that we do the same for Facebook videos.

Time is everything

Researchers compared the performance of over 100 million native Facebook videos and found that the top performing video posts were the ones that were 60 - 90 seconds long. The second best-performing ones were 90-120 seconds long, and the third spot went to those that were between 30 and 60 seconds. Essentially, viewers are more interested in shorter videos since the Internet has bred a culture of impatience amongst its users.

Viewers like their information served fast and don't appreciate delays and long spans of video footage that eat up too much of their time. Fortunately for these picky viewers, Facebook allows users to see how long a video is by hovering over it as it plays. If users see that it lasts more than a minute and a half, interest declines by nearly one third, and the other two-thirds scroll away in search of something less taxing to watch.

<u>Sound isn't necessary</u>

Starting in the fall of 2017, Facebook decided to change the way it played videos by turning the sound off from the start of the video, leaving the viewer the discretion of turning it on if they want to. Since then, a whopping 90% of their videos are played without sound, leaving some marketers in the mud when it comes to delivering a message and retaining customers.

Unfortunately, if you share key information on your videos through audio alone, many viewers will choose to ditch it in favor of posts that are easier to understand and enjoy even in the absence of sound. For this reason, Facebook encourages businesses to generate video content that uses captions and graphics to deliver the information.

Of course, you can add some music or audio to your videos to cater to those that still prefer watching the old-fashioned way, but it's best to make sure that you're not communicating all of the essentials of your marketing message with audio alone. In the end, people would still rather read than listen, since it offers better privacy especially in public or shared spaces.

<u>Hook at the start</u>

When posting a video, another factor to take into consideration is the fact that users will scroll away if they don't find it interesting right from the start. How soon do they decide that they're not interested, you ask? According to statistics, all it takes is 4 seconds. If after that period, you don't hook them with your content, they're not likely to stay.

Powerful copy delivered at the get-go can make it more likely for viewers to complete the video. Combined with potent imagery, this information can fuel interest and keep viewers hooked until you deliver your punch line. Take the example of 5-Minute Crafts - a viral Facebook page that offers its viewers quick, easy, and simple strategies to make beautiful handicraft projects that require neither a lot of time or money. The page also provides short clips on everyday hacks that their viewers can use to remedy a variety of household and personal inconveniences.

Scanning through the page's videos, you'll notice one thing about the majority of them - they combine eye-catching images with interesting captions right off the bat, making their viewers wonder - how do they do it?

Squeezing the juice out of an apple, for example, is one of their uncommon yet clever kitchen hacks. Most would think it is impossible, but the fact that the page says otherwise within the first few seconds of the video makes people want to stick around to find out how it's really done.

You'll notice that the video itself is nearly 4 minutes long. So, what happened to the rule of time? That's the beauty of relevance - if you've established your business well enough as a reliable and relevant source of information, your viewers won't care how long your videos are and will likely sit through the entire thing, especially if you're known for the value and uniqueness of the information you share.

Paid Video Ads

Ad placement on Facebook is mainly divided into two possible categories: photos and videos. Photo ads are simple. They're published in the feed in between other items from friends and liked pages. This creates continuity and relieves the user from the inconvenience of being bombarded with pop-up ads that are often unwanted and inconvenient. Other than that, photo ads can also be placed along a side panel on the desktop version of Facebook, and between conversations in the Messenger App.

As part of its Terms and Conditions, as well as its user protection policy, Facebook labels these posts as "Sponsored" to prevent confusion amongst its users, since they may be mistaken for friends' posts or liked pages' publications. They're also formatted slightly differently compared to typical stories you would see on your feed.

Along the bottom of the ad, you'll see a CTA button that helps make it easier for viewers to access the content being advertised. This changes from ad to ad and ultimately depends on what you feel might benefit your business most effectively.

One other way that video ads differ from their photo ad counterparts is that they can be squeezed into video publications from other pages. Why? Well, with the dense population that Facebook has and the increasing demand for ad placement, the platform had to come up with new places to allow its businesses' ads to show. So, in August of 2017, Facebook started allowing marketers to add in-stream video ads to viral posts throughout the platform.

There are a few parameters that Facebook sets when it decides where in-stream ads can show up. For instance, published videos need to reach a certain length and specific engagement metrics to qualify for ad placement. This helps guarantee that shorter videos don't become compounded with in-stream videos that could dampen their efficacy and the goal of the short span. On top of that, Facebook chooses only top performing content from the highest quality publishers to add in-stream video ads too.

By doing this, the platform helps improve ad viewership and

completion. The better the video publications perform, the more likely they're of interest to a wider scope of users and viewers.

Based on Facebook standards, in-stream video ads need to be between 5-15 seconds in length, but the platform recommends that businesses try to stick to the shorter end of the spectrum to keep viewers hooked. Out of 100 in-stream ads, 30 push viewers scroll to the next story despite the original video's quality and high level of engagement. That's because the video ads themselves might not have rubbed off the right way on the viewer, causing them to abandon ship even if they were genuinely interested in the initial video they were watching.

Finally, it's important to point out another factor on in-stream ad completion which is the user's internet connection. Of course, that's something neither you nor Facebook has the power to control. But if your viewers' connections are unstable and slow, they may choose to scroll past a video once it shows an ad especially if it's too long for their preference.

Longer ad videos take longer to load, and individuals with slow internet connections don't want to waste their time on social media waiting for ads to play. If you're considering this variable, you might want to shorten your videos to increase viewership and completion, so you can send your message across - even to users that might not have the best internet speeds.

Likes

If there's one main concept you need to keep in mind for this next section, it's that on Facebook, likes are currency. The more likes your page has, the higher its market value. Also, the more likes your posts have, the farther they'll reach.

Statistics have found that Facebook pages with more likes

tend to outperform their competition. The reason is two-fold:

Reputation

Buyers associate more likes with a better reputation. Surveys conducted amongst consumers discovered that Facebook users are more inclined to purchase goods or use the services of businesses that have more likes. This is associated with a "good reputation", since a brand that doesn't meet consumer preferences or standards is unlikely to collect as many likes.

More likes

More likes equals better quality. Consider the case of Business A and Business B - both specializing in third-party grocery delivery services. Both businesses buy your groceries for you and deliver them to your doorstep the same day. They also both operate within the same area, so they're pretty much competing for the same audience.

A first-time customer might check out both of their pages since they're well known in the community. Business A has 100,000 likes while Business B has 75,000. On its own, the value of 75,000 might seem big enough, but since this consumer is comparing, they'd likely choose the business with more page likes because it is likely to offer more efficient quality services.

Essentially, the more likes you have, the more likely people will see your business as a worthy, reputable, and trustworthy entity to deal with. Of course, the initial problem pages face when it comes to likes is how to get them in the first place. Since Facebook users are more inclined to liking a page that already has likes to begin with, how does a page with zero likes get the ball rolling? There are a few tactics you might want to try out.

Invite Your Friends

Remember how your Facebook page is linked to your profile? This opens up the opportunity to easily get likes even if your business is relatively unknown. On your page, you'll see a side panel that gives you the option to invite your friends to like your page. For small business owners, this is often the most accessible way to start getting likes, since your friends probably already know that you're trying to kickstart your brand.

When your friends give your page a like, Facebook may publish it as a story on your friends' feed. So, your page could cause a blip in second-and third-degree friends' radars, especially if many of your common friends also like it. The result? You instantly extend your reach and get a positive impression amongst people in your circle. People think that "if my friends like this page, then it must be a good product or service provider."

Add a Call to Action on Your Website

Some SME's with dedicated business websites might be able to draw in more traffic to their page if they include a "Like" button on their blog or home page. Doing so makes it easier for website viewers to find you on Facebook and promises them access to more relevant and important content that they do not want to miss out on. If you use other social media platforms for your business, such as Instagram or Twitter, it's a good idea to include a link to them on your Facebook page as well.

Pay for Ads

There's a lot to learn about paid ads, and we will discuss this in greater detail in later chapters. For now, it's worth mentioning that paid ads can boost your reach much more dramatically, especially if you're willing to spend more. A great example is Weekly World News - a Facebook Page that jumped from 3,224 likes to 40,310 likes in a matter of 4 days, all thanks to the power of paid advertising.

As a relatively new Facebook entity, you may want to consider paying extra to achieve visibility in more people's feeds. Don't worry - if you're only just starting, you might not need to pay more than a couple of bucks to reach your intended audience. As you grow, and competition becomes more aggressive, it might be important to add more to your paid advertisement budget.

Tactics to Avoid

We've all seen those ultra-popular Facebook pages that seem like they don't deserve the number of likes they've somehow "earned" on the platform. How did they do it? Often, these questionable pages had to use a few sly and unorthodox tricks to be able to cheat and act like they're widely popular. While it might be enticing to do the same, these methods are highly discouraged since they don't draw in the kind of audience you want.

Fake Promotions with Branded Names

Some brands - especially big multinational ones - might have different Facebook pages to cater to specific countries. For instance, McDonald's has numerous Facebook pages, each one providing country-specific offers and promotions that are relevant to the people they serve. In some cases, there might even be smaller Facebook pages for each country that the brand operates in. So, McDonald's Ontario could have a unique page separate from McDonald's Canada. This is what some Facebook businesses have tried to exploit - the fact that some large companies can have multiple official pages at any given time.

While this was intended to make it easier for consumers to access relevant, local information and assistance, it has somehow backfired. Some business owners have gone as far as opening fraudulent Facebook pages that pose as supportive pages for bigger companies. That parade as ancillary pages for large corporations. Then, these pages promote themselves with fake promotions, claiming to give away a prize at the end of the offer period. All participants have to do is - you guessed it - comment on and share their promotional post.

These spread like wildfire, especially because most giveaway prizes are out of this world, including cars, large sums of money, and all-expenses-paid holidays. Since not many people are aware of the scam, they end up engaging and spreading the promotion throughout the platform, allowing the page to gain momentum and collect thousands of likes in a matter of days.

Once the page owner gets the number of likes they want, they quickly change their identity and erase all previous posts. This is also why a lot of Facebook users are often surprised to see a bunch of liked pages that they have no recollection of.

The reason why this method doesn't work is that the likes generated aren't targeted. There is no specific audience, so once you shift to your actual product or service, there's no guarantee that the likes you've generated will translate to conversions.

Plus, once those users start seeing posts you publish on their News Feed, they're likely to quickly unlike your page, since they don't think it's relevant to their likes and preferences.

Buying Likes

If you've got the money to spend, why not just buy Facebook likes? Hey, it's possible. These services promise to bump up the number of likes your page receives in a short time frame, which often gains the attention of business owners who want fast growth. Unfortunately, buying likes is a temporary solution and the likes generated aren't likely to produce the outcome you want. Why?

Consider Business X - a small, start-up enterprise that offers roof replacement services in Portland. They engage about 8-10% of their audience with their posts, generating quite a bit of discussion in the comments section and receiving a reasonable number of likes on each newly published post. Currently, they have 1,000 organic likes that they have collected in 6 months.

Now, the business wants to increase its number of likes, thinking it will improve its online reputation and bring in more consumers. The owner pays a third-party service to collect more likes, which they fulfill. In a matter of a few weeks, the page already has 2,300 likes.

Unfortunately, after purchasing the likes, the engagement was close to 0% and comments and likes quickly died down. About a month after the service, the page was essentially dead, generating zero traffic and struggling to produce any real interaction from its audience.

What happened? The purchased likes came from all over the

globe, with the majority coming from Africa since the service doesn't pick out Facebook profiles that matter to your business. Now, most of the business's posts landed on these irrelevant Facebook users who were unlikely to share, comment, or like these posts. After all, how could you get an African citizen to be interested in your roofing services all the way in Portland?

Keep in mind that organic reach on Facebook is tough since there are millions of businesses that fight for the same spotlight. So, Facebook will only give your posts exposure to a maximum of 12% of your audience. Because Business X's audience mainly came from Africa, these fake followers likely took up the maximum reach allotment Facebook would allow per post.

The result? Zero movement, zero engagement, and unfortunately, zero conversions.

Unlimited Posting

When it comes to Facebook marketing, they say that content is king, so does that mean you can post an unlimited number of pictures, informational snippets, and videos in a day, and you'll get the engagement you want?

Unfortunately, spamming your Facebook fans with posts won't generate the likes you want either. Pages that post too often and end up eating up a user's entire News Feed will be considered a nuisance, and they might lead to some people unliking the page altogether. Also, because Facebook ultimately gets to decide how often, and on which feeds your posts pop up, it's unlikely that all your publications will appear where you want them to.

When posting anything on Facebook, the ultimate rule is quality over quantity. Sometimes, a good post will spend several months in circulation if it hits all the right notes with your audience.

Getting Likes

Now that you've got a couple of hundred likes on your page, there are a few things you can try to bump those numbers up even more. These tactics are intended to help you reach an actual, relevant audience, so you can expect consistent engagement and hopefully, reliable conversions.

Enlist the help of an Internet personality. They're not Hollywood celebrities, but Internet personalities have changed the way people enjoy entertainment. Usually, these people have large follower bases that engage aggressively with their posts. They're popular because they have skills that others hope to have, or because they live lives that their fans desire. Internet personalities such as travel bloggers, make-up artists, food critics, and fashion gurus all post on social media for a living.

The first step to figuring out who you should ask to team up with you is to understand your brand, as you'll want to get help from someone who resonates with it. Take the example of Bretman Rock - a fun, quirky male makeup artist who achieved Internet stardom by way of his edgy makeup style that contrasts dramatically with his masculine look. He was taken on by Benefit Cosmetics - a contemporary makeup brand that leverages a fun, colorful aesthetic and appeals to consumers with its meme culture personality. Together, the two made millions in sales.

Choosing the right influencer can help bring more attention to your brand, especially because an influencer's follower base typically deeply trusts their recommendations. So, if Bretman Rock were to recommend a product from Benefit Cosmetics, his

10.7 million Instagram followers wouldn't second-guess his opinion and take it at face value. For Benefit Cosmetics, that means the possibility of 10.7 million guaranteed buyers.

Once you've pinpointed a viable influencer to work with, reach out to them with your offer. Typically, these individuals aren't seeking monetary compensation and would be happy to post positively about your brand with nothing more than a freebie or free service. Sending a care package of your items their way gives them material to work with, so they can generate the content you need to drive traffic to your Facebook Page.

In some cases, influencers also team up with brands to host a giveaway for their followers. The Internet personality will ultimately be in charge of signal boosting your brand during the giveaway period. This helps guarantee that your brand reaches the audience your chosen influencer has built through their popularity.

How does the promotion convert to page likes? Easy - request all giveaway participants to like your Facebook page. If you have chosen an internet blogger that fits your niche, the people that liked it will likely stay even after the giveaway is over out of interest for the products and services that you offer.

Generate Quality Content

Share-worthy content is the number one method to attract more likes on your page. When you post, you have the potential to reach 12% (on a good day) of your intended audience. When a page follower shares your post, the odds of it reaching a larger audience's feed increases. The more people share what you post, the wider your reach becomes, allowing you to earn a spot on the feed of Facebook users who don't yet know your brand.

There are also specific times in the day when your post will probably get the most engagement. So, trying to meet those schedules by posting one quality piece during the hour when traffic is highest can help improve post engagement and performance.

If you consistently post share-worthy content, you grow your chance of reaching more people. In effect, you can increase the number of likes you have over a short period. Take Buzzfeed's Tasty, for example - a food and drink page that focuses on providing its viewers with quick and easy meal prep recipes in video form. Their posts are typically highly visual, making the whole process of cooking an enticing dream. Users share their content either to bookmark the recipes or to share them with friends. Currently, Tasty has earned a whopping 95 million likes on their page, which has opened new opportunities for them including affiliate marketing and cookbook publication.

Stick around - one great post doesn't guarantee lifelong returns. Facebook churns out some 2.5 billion posts a day, processing 500 + terabytes worth of data daily. Given those numbers, even your best performing posts might not last long enough on the platform and easily fizzle out into the background as new content is published. Sure, it will always be available on your page, but if you're not present on your users' feed, you might struggle to get new likes.

Consistent, scheduled posting can help maintain your presence alongside your competition. By regularly generating content and publishing it on your page, you'll keep popping up on the feed to reach new prospective buyers.

Step 8: Facebook Ads

Ads are what companies use to advertise their products or services on Facebook. As mentioned earlier, it is important for companies to put out information about their products, so more people are made aware of it.

These Facebook ads are mostly displayed on the right corner, but you can choose where to place them on the page. You can do so by changing the settings.

You can read about Facebook ads by accessing the "Facebook ads guide", where you can educate yourself on the "Types of Ads" that can be created. Here are some of the choices you will find:

· Click to website - this will take you directly to the website.

· Review design recommendations - you can review the designs that can be incorporated in the ads

· Carousel - the carousel will help your audience view multiple products and services at once

· You can add in tracking to see how many leads you have captured

· It is important to leave behind a "call-to-action" option that your audience can click on to take appropriate action

There is a big difference between the ads that play on the website and the ones on the app, so you have to customize the ads to fit well with the app. Here are the steps you should take to do so:

· You must first install the app and have a clear idea of what ads will look like on it.

· Next, you must see how engaged your audience will be.

· You need to be aware of the local events and happenings to appeal to your audience.

- You should keep track of other companies' offers and try to compete with them as much as possible.
- Remember that it is important to distinguish between your website views and mobile views.

To check the ads before they go live, you can use a video testing tool.

Basics of Facebook Advertising

Facebook advertising is a very powerful tool that you can use to promote your products and services. Advertising on Facebook is very easy once you know how to go about it. Here is how you can get started with it.

Once you have your ad permit, go to the "manage your ads" button on Facebook.com/adsmanage

Once there, pick the options you would like to incorporate in your ads feature. If you wish to create an ad from scratch, follow the following steps:

- Choose the type of ad that you wish to control. This depends on what you want the ad to stand for.
- Next, choose the objective of your campaign and incorporate it in the ad as extensively as possible.
- Next, choose the demographic that the ad will be displayed to. Doing so will help your ad better connect with the chosen audience.
- Next, decide on the budget that you wish to allot for the ad. It pays to have a number in mind as it helps you stay on track to prevent overspending. You can set the budget based on how big you want the ad to be.
- Next, you must create an audience for your ads. You should always remember who the audience that will be viewing your

ads is and incorporate elements that will please them.

Creating a Page Like Ad

- When it comes to creating a Facebook ad, you have to follow a few steps.
- You can start by creating the ad
- Remember, it is important to promote your Facebook page so that more and more people have the chance to see your ads
- Just like a page, it's important to set a budget for your video ads. If you don't set a budget, you run the risk of over-shooting it
- It is important to pick the right demographics in order for the ad to make a big impact. If you create an ad that does not appeal to the chosen demographic, it will end up just being a wasteful campaign
- It is important to choose the right campaign name for your ad as it will greatly help to capture your audience's attention
- You must make use of thoughtful pictures that work well with your chosen audience

Creating Audiences

It is no secret that your ads will not work if you don't create an appropriate audience for it. Here is what you can do to deal with that:

- You can click on the audience tab to choose the right audience for your work
- You can customize the audience that you already know and pick out people who best suit your campaign
- You can choose where your audience comes from. For

example, it can be from your friends' list or your Facebook page

· You can upload a list of people, import them or pick out specific people from your list of friends

· Next, you should agree to Facebook's terms and conditions

· It is best to name your audience so that you know what they comprise of, for example, if it is a group of teenagers, you can name it "teens."

· It is a good idea to test your ad with a dummy audience to see if it clicks

· Once you create the ad, you can import your audience over

· You can upload appropriate images to suit your ad campaign

· You can choose how long the ad will run on Facebook

· Remember that all the ads go through a screening process, so it is best to preview the ad before going live

· It is extremely important to create an audience for all your ads

· You can save a target group and name it to create specific ads for them

· The target groups will be chosen based on demographics

· You can generate a graph that will show you the size of the demographics

· It is best to try the ad out on an audience to make sure that it is driving across the right message

Creating Facebook Ads

1. Click on the create ads tab

2. Choose the objective of the ad

3. Add the name of the campaign

4. You can either choose an audience or create one from scratch. You can also import an audience from your page

5. It is vital to add demographics to capture the right audience

6. You can pick the options to add in multiple images or a single image

7. You can always connect to your Facebook page

8. You can click on the languages tab to pick the language of choice

9. It is extremely important to add in a call to action to help people take the right course of action

10. You can generate a conversation tracker to keep tab of your conversations

11. It is best to name your ad campaign to facilitate future reference

12. You should keep track of the page views

13. Make note of the URL

14. You have to validate the ad that you create

15. You can edit your ad by clicking on the "campaigns" tab

16. You can use an old ad to serve as a base for another ad by switching the images

17. You can keep the basic concept of the ad intact and work on the images used

Video Ads

Video ads are much better than picture ads as they are better at capturing your audience's attention. Here are steps you can follow to create video ads:

· Start by creating a plan for the ad

· Next, just as you would for your regular ads, choose your target audience, as you will have to choose the right demographics for your video ads

· Next, you have to choose the budget for the ad. Like with

regular ads, it is best to set aside a budget as it will help you stay on course.

· You should upload a video that has the specifications of 720p, and a ratio of 16x9

· You must preview the ad before going live so that you can make any changes to it if needed

Reports

It is important to look at reports to understand how your ads are faring. Here is how you can do so. Start by clicking on the "reports" tab present on the left side.

There, you will find the following options:

· General metrics

· Choose demographics to look at

· Export as excel file

· You can pick the cost per click option to see how much you are making through the clicks on your ads

· You can filter the results to see what is working well for you and what isn't

· If you have hired a team to look into the analytics, you can add people if you want them to have access to the account and make the desired changes.

· You can put an email notification if you want to be notified for clicks.

· You can always access account history to peek into the history of your account.

Remember that it is important for you to treat your Facebook page as the primary tool to communicate with your audience and update them on the company's latest developments. Do not get carried away and start posting things that are of a personal nature. It is also best not to get into arguments with anyone that posts on your page. You can hire a team to answer customer queries and try to post new content as frequently as possible.

It is important to stay enthusiastic and not allow the page to go cold.

Get a Custom Advertising Plan

For marketers who aren't sure what would work best for their business, Facebook offers the option of getting a custom plan. To start, the platform asks a series of questions about your business. These include how you make sales (physical vs. virtual), whether it's necessary for your prospects to communicate with you to initiate a purchase, and how you'd like them to reach out to you.

In this sample suggested plan, Facebook found that the business would benefit most from an advertisement that collects contact information since sales were initiated by the brand reaching out to the consumers instead of the other way around. After that, you can create your form to help collect contacts to fuel conversions for your business. This changes depending on the result from result to result and some suggested plans would require a completely different CTA or format, depending on the outcomes of the questionnaire.

Working with guided advertising experience can help users determine the best marketing strategy for their Facebook page. The promotion allows up to 6 different ads and makes it possible for users to choose between a single image for their ad, a video, or a multi-products ad format.

Promote Your Business Locally

For service providers or businesses that sell large items, it is ideal to target a local audience. The option to promote your business locally makes it possible to achieve more sales at your actual store - a benefit sought out by most small businesses with brick-and-mortars. For instance, a small dental clinic might use this ad to reach for a relevant audience near its store to attract more new patients.

As you click on the option to promote your business locally, Facebook offers a few settings that can be adjusted to better meet your needs. These include the distance of the users you'd like to reach defined by a radius around your listed business address, the age, gender, and interests of your target audience and the copy that you want with your ad.

Users also have the option to include a map to make it easier for their audience to locate them. Along the side panel of the ad configuration pane, the platform shows a preview of the ad on the Facebook desktop feed, mobile, and Instagram.

Finally, marketers also have the option to choose their daily budget. Depending on the size of your business and the extent of the reach you want to achieve with your ad, you may want to adjust your budget accordingly. As we've discussed in an earlier chapter, a bigger budget doesn't necessarily mean better returns. Find your sweet spot and stick to it until you notice a dramatic and sustained increase in your metrics.

Promote Your Page

Some businesses or brands make conversions with their content. Take, for example, the Goodful Page from Buzzfeed, which makes commissions off of affiliate marketing content that makes conversions. They present the products through their viral video and provide a link for viewers to purchase it if they are interested. They also have their own line-up of household essentials that Facebook users can learn more about on their page.

So naturally, driving traffic to their Facebook page is necessary to increase sales and improve the ROI of their brand. In this case, ads that promote page popularity become an integral part of the Facebook marketing strategy.

Just like the ads that promote your business locally, these ads can be targeted to users of a specific age, gender, and area, and they can be set to show an image, a video, or multiple products that viewers can swipe through. However, the CTA button can only be set to Like the business's page, and the publications are limited to Facebook. These ads can show up on the feed and on the side panel of the Facebook website on desktop.

Promoting your Facebook page with ads like these can be incredibly beneficial if your brand communicates most of its messages through its page. For affiliate marketers and viral news pages, this type of ad often proves to be most effective.

Promote Your Website

These ads are ideal for businesses and service providers that use their website more actively than their pages. For instance, Upwork - a freelancing platform that connects businesses with independent professionals – performs all of its functions through its website. This is where users log in, interact with clients and freelancers, and get paid. So, anyone who might want to use Upwork needs to access their website to get the most out of the platform's benefits and functions. On the other hand, the purpose of their Facebook presence is simple – to draw more users to their website.

For that purpose, Upwork's Facebook ads are mostly formatted to drive more website traffic. These ads work pretty much the same way that the previous ads do, except that they use a Learn More CTA that brings Facebook users to their website if they click.

Get More Leads

Consider RISE – Europe's largest tech conference that attracts some 70,000 participants from over 170 countries all over the globe. The Web Summit aims to bring together the latest trends in e-commerce and tech and invites key speakers to share the stories and experiences behind some of the most successful start-ups in the whole world. For events enterprises like RISE, ads that get leads are most important. Why? By collecting contact information from people that might be interested in their event, they can deliver more powerful copy through select communication channels to entice prospects to sign up. This powerful marketing method also increases long-term engagement which might be beneficial to other types of businesses since it gives them the opportunity to keep re-using contact information for future promotions.

Zalora – a popular clothing marketplace offers brands both old and new the chance to reach their market through their dedicated retail website and app. It uses lead advertising to collect user information and emails in order to send them promotional copy in the future. In exchange for giving out your info, Zalora's lead advertisements share exclusive coupon codes for discounts on their platform.

For most users, it's a reasonable exchange. For business owners, it helps with future engagement and conversions by creating a permanent audience base that's willing to hear what they have to say and share. Of course, in the future, the newsletters and information you send should be worthy of engagement, but that's a whole other topic.

Chapter Five: Delivering Value to Audience and Growing your Business

In this section, we will look at posting schedules and quality and providing value to your mailing list as it grows.

Step 9 : Posting Relevancy and Quality

It's time to discuss the basics of posting on Facebook. On your page, you have access to pretty much the same posting features that personal profiles have, with a few business exclusive extras. Learning how to leverage each one will help empower your Facebook marketing strategy and improve the returns you get from using the social media platform.

Before we dive into each one of these options, it's important to discuss the ideal frequency and timing. These two facets of Facebook posting will largely affect the performance of your content and may even determine whether or not they'll be beneficial to your business at all.

Timing refers to the hour of the day that you choose to publish your post. As a business, you need to understand that your target market might have a preferred time for social media depending on their availability.

For instance, Business Y, which sells Littman stethoscopes,

might find that they have a large audience during graveyard hours. These are possibly doctors, nurses, and other medical professionals that open their Facebook apps while reporting for night duty. Business Z, on the other hand, caters to rank and file workers and may have increased engagement after 5 PM on weekdays, since that's when their target market is online.

Understanding your market's schedule will help make it easier for you to be present while they're available. This increases the chances of discovery and helps keep you present amongst all Facebook content.

Post at the time of day when your fans are online – you can check this on your page's insights. Posting during the peak of audience availability should give your posts a greater chance of landing on the Feed. Posting during down hours or too long before peak hours could push your post further down the feed, especially if more relevant friends and pages post after you do.

Of course, there are benefits to posting during down times too, especially if you notice that there are still some users online at that time. Remember that if you're trying to compete with other brands, they're likely vying for the attention of the same audience, which means they're probably going to post at the same hours that you are.

If brands in one niche all post at the same time, the odds that Facebook's algorithm will allow all of you to appear on your audience's feed are very slim. Facebook knows that users like variety, so if they've already posted one brand that sells products or services similar to yours, they might not include your post until after a couple of hundred others.

Having said that, there is something to gain from posting during limited audience availability since your competitors would probably be more focused on the primetime spot. The

CHAPTER FIVE: DELIVERING VALUE TO AUDIENCE AND GROWING YOUR...

delicate balance, however, lies in how often you decide to post during these hours.

Frequency is another facet to Facebook posting that can help your business secure a regular spot on your audience's news feed. Posting too much drives away readers and possible buyers because it floods their News Feed with content that comes from the same place. Facebook users like variety, so if they keep getting blips from you instead of other pages and people they might find relevant, they could cut you out to make room for others on their feed.

According to experts, daily posting should be limited to 2, and your weekly total should not be more than ten. This feeds your fans a steady flow of relevant information to keep your brand present in their social media plane and helps keep you from fading away into the background in the fight against your competitors.

Let's say you choose to stick to the rules and post twice a day - when should you post? Experts recommend posting one during peak audience hours, and another during non-peak hours, preferably at the start of the day. Even if there are a few posts from similar pages published after you've posted yours, your post still the chance to float around the website and land on people's Feeds before the day ends.

How do you know if your scheduling is working? This is where the handy analytics feature for Facebook businesses comes in handy. On your insights Page, you'll see all the posts you've ever published listed in chronological order, with the newest one at the top. Next to each post is information on how it performed in terms of engagement and reach.

Of course, the content of the post will play a role in its overall performance, but you might be able to detect a pattern by comparing how posts during certain hours perform compared to those posted during other times of the day.

Facebook is fundamentally based on posts and their ability to go 'viral', so your aim is for your post to be so encapsulating that it draws people in. Here are some tips and tricks to make your Facebook posts go viral:

Use Emotions

Facebook is not really about selling products – it's actually about connecting with people, and you can't do that unless you sell emotions. So, it doesn't matter what your product is, if you want people to care about your page and your brand, you have to connect with them emotionally.

The only way that you can connect with people is by blending the utility of your product with things that people can relate with. So, if you're trying to sell clothes, for example, you can't just show people what you're selling and hope that they wear it. Instead, if you put up a story of how your clothes are made and the people that work endlessly to ensure that the clothes are perfect, you're far more likely to gain public attention.

Don't Overdo It

Of course, trying to connect with your potential audience is important, but make sure that you're not trying too hard. If you continue to latch on to every new trend and keep on making jokes, it's eventually going to saturate your audience. Also, many brands think that they can connect to the younger generation by using their slang and style, but try not to partake in silly things like this, as it's only going to make your posts seem forced and fake.

At the end of the day, it's important to remember that you're selling something. If you're going to try your hardest to make it seem otherwise, it's only going to make your audience unreactive to what you have to say.

Keep Posts Short & Specific

The one key role in Facebook marketing is to keep your customer's attention – if your customer sees posts that are too long and all your posts are videos, they're not going to engage much.

Be honest with the audience and be open with them about what you're selling while at the same time trying to connect with them. Most brands tend to have far more success with shorter posts than they do with huge advertisement campaigns, but if you do decide to have longer posts, remember to add pictures and paragraphs. This will at least make your audience interested enough to continue reading.

Visual

According to statistics, posts that include images produce 650% higher engagement than their text-only counterparts. This part of online consumer culture was born with the ease and speed of the internet, making people opt for faster, less taxing ways of getting their information. So, text that's placed over an image as opposed to text alone can grab attention and cause more aggressive engagement.

Of course, using just any image won't do. Studies have found that images that look cluttered and confusing tend to push consumers away since people don't want to have to guess what your post is trying to say.

Having said that - one of the cornerstones of quality content is high quality, eye-catching images. No matter whether it's a sale, a change of office schedule, a promotional offer, new products in your line-up, and everything in between, publishing the announcement in the form of an image can significantly improve its performance.

Informational or Interesting

To be classified as a quality post, Your Facebook post has to be one of two things. First, it has to be informational - that is, it provides readers with details that they wouldn't have otherwise known. Second, it has to be interesting - while it might not be new information, it can be presented in a way that grabs attention.

A great example of a Facebook Page that leverages informational content is Ted-Ed. Focused on providing their viewers with highly visual, beautifully animated, short video snippets that share new perspectives on educational lessons, Ted-Ed has become a major entertainment hub for those who want chunks of information that are a little more on the intellectual side.

An example of a page that posts interesting content is Insider Presents, who has 3.4 million likes. This page features short videos relating to travel, food, culture, and other interesting tidbits from all over the globe. Their videos typically go viral, and the information is rarely ever new, but because of the way they present their stories, they've become a major entertainment hub for Facebook users who want to use their free time to learn interesting new information.

Apps for Business Marketing

To be more successful, there are various apps that every Facebook marketer must have. These apps are not officially made by Facebook but are meant to help you run your business page on Facebook.

These apps are pretty straightforward, but at the same time, they will help you to manage your page even better. They will track progress and help you with the content on your page, and are a must-have for anyone who is running a business Facebook page.

Custom Tab Apps

These are the kind of apps that help you install a small website on your Facebook page. With the help of these apps, you can have customized videos, images, etc on a single tab. These apps are extremely helpful because not everybody has brilliant editing and computer skills - if you are one of these people, then these apps will do everything for you in order to give your customers everything that they might need. Recommendations: Hayo and Tabsite.

Email capture apps

Email capture apps are apps that will help you get the email addresses of your Facebook audience without disturbing them. It can be really difficult to get peoples' email addresses, but you need them to expand your reach. You can get the email address from the people who visit your page by making them click on certain links, so you don't have to ask for email addresses directly. Recommendations: Constant Contact and AWeber.

Quiz and Poll apps

These are the kind of apps that help in preparing polls and surveys to post on your page. Quizzes and polls are an important way to gain customer feedback, because the more customer feedback you have, the better you can serve your customers. For this purpose, you need apps because it's really difficult to get people interested in taking a short survey or quiz. Quiz and Poll apps ensure that whatever you create is suitable enough to easily attract people. Recommendations: Woobox and Antavo.

Automatic Posting apps

Automatic posting apps are a savior for anyone who does not have the time to regularly update their business's Facebook page. It is available on Facebook, where it lets you create a post now and scheduling the exact time when you want it to appear. This is helpful because not everyone has the time to post regularly on their page and if you don't, your page starts to look dead, which gives a very bad impression to any customer who visits it. Scheduled posting ensures that your page seems active even when you are too busy to post anything. This can be done directly on Facebook itself, while some apps can also do it for you. Recommendations: Buffer and Rignite.

Social Media Integration apps

Social media integration is the concept of being able to use different social media sites with the help of just one app. By using these apps, you can connect different social media sites to your Facebook page, so that whatever you post on other social media sites also appears on your Facebook page. So, with the help of Social Media Integration apps, when you post something on your Twitter or your Instagram, it will automatically be posted on your Facebook page. You get a lot of benefit out of this because many users follow a couple of social media sites exclusively, and they might connect with you on other social media platforms if they see your Facebook posts. Recommendations: Pagemodo and Tabsite.

Contest apps

Contests apps help you to organize contests on your Facebook page to increase participation and keep your audience interested. Contests take a lot of effort and can be difficult to organize; you even have to check the terms and conditions that Facebook has laid out for them. You can deal with all of this with the help of Contest apps because they make it easier for you to organize a contest, making sure that you comply with Facebook's terms and conditions. Recommendations: Offerpop and Votigo.

Chapter Six: Monetizing your Business

In this part, you will learn how to monetize your business by selling your products, as well as how to monetize Facebook groups.

Step 10 : Selling on Facebook

Back when the concepts of online marketing and social media marketing were in their infancy, marketers were scrambling to find ways to get their audience from Facebook to their dedicated web pages. More often than not, SMEs would have a website before any social media page because, at the time, social media platforms weren't seen as a basic need for a marketing strategy. As time went on, pre-established websites had more information on them, and it just seemed practical to ask people to visit websites instead of trying to pack Facebook pages with the same amount of information.

Unfortunately, it was easy to see that this specific method wasn't working out for a large chunk of the market. Buyers are already where they want to be - on Facebook. So, asking them to get off their comfort zone and into your web page was often seen as impractical and tedious - especially if other similar brands in the market offer pretty much the same thing without asking them to leave Facebook.

Of course, the good folk at Facebook realized this, too, so they decided to make it easier for sellers to market their products and generate sales from Facebook itself. That's when the Shop Section was born.

As a unique Facebook business page feature, the Shop section allows marketers to post listings on their page to offer products or services for sale. For any business that's anchored on revenue, this is one of the most important aspects of the Facebook marketing strategy, leading you to an actual opportunity to do what you've been aiming to do all along - generate sales.

You can find the Shop option along the left-hand panel of your page, bunched together with the other options that Facebook offers. When you click it, you'll be asked to agree to Merchant Terms and Policies. Then, it's as simple as choosing how buyers can make a purchase and deciding the currency of your shop.

Message to Buy means the users would have to go through the Messenger app to make a purchase. It's a manual process that needs your response to go ahead. Check Out on Another Website redirects users to your e-commerce web page where they can purchase your item outside of Facebook. Since not many small businesses have a dedicated e-commerce page, Message to Buy is often a more practical solution.

Once all of that is done, Facebook gives you the option to start posting your items for sale. The process entails filling out a pop-up form that requires some information on your product to give buyers specific details on what you offer.

When you click save, you will get a pop-up that tells you that your product post has been submitted for review.

After a few minutes, your new item should be ready and viewable on your Shop Section. This requirement is a necessary part of Facebook's process as the platform wants to ensure that all listings follow their strict rules and guidelines

Facebook gives page owners the option to post an unrestricted number of items on their page and the opportunity for marketers to create collections so that buyers can browse items effortlessly. Once there are items in your shop, your page also gets the Shop widget added to the home page. This makes it easier for prospects to see what you sell, and it empowers profitable consumer action.

When it comes to its selling facet, the only flaw that Facebook has is that it doesn't have a payment center, which means that it still isn't an e-commerce platform. So, buyers who message you to inquire about your items will have to be provided other payment channels such as PayPal or online bank transfers that still require them to leave the platform.

However, the beauty of the Facebook shop is that it hooks your audience more securely so that they feel compelled to make a purchase. As they continue to explore your page, learn your story, see your identity, and of course, browse your items, they begin to want your products more, making the tedious process of leaving Facebook worth it.

While we can only dream of the day that Facebook adds payments to its list of features, there are a few other things you can do while waiting. The following techniques help make generating sales more seamless and effortless, letting you boost profitable consumer action through your Facebook page to bump up revenue and make all those marketing efforts worth it.

Don't Overdo It

Imagine having lunch with a few friends at the mall, before a solicitor sits down at your table to share some information on a product or service he's trying to sell. You politely ask him to leave, but he says that he will, but only after you've checked out his offers. What do you think your next move would be? Probably to get up and go away. Whatever he was trying to sell; you've definitely got a bad impression of it permanently ingrained in your brain.

In the same light, people on Facebook aren't here to be sold to. They're here to have a good time, socialize, learn, and share what they find interesting. So, pushing your items on them too aggressively could mean pushing them away from your brand and giving them the wrong impression altogether.

While it would be smart to keep your products and promotional offers constantly updated, focusing only on revenue leaves a bad impression on your audience, especially if you're not sharing any relevant, informational, or interesting content in between. Consider spending one day of the week updating sale information, and the rest of the week engaging your audience.

Emphasize Use

Most prospective buyers respond best to brands that show them how products can be used. That's why influencers become so effective - because they show their audience how to style a top, a pair of pants, or a fresh take on a new pair of designer heels. Their fashion inspires and makes their viewers think, "Hey, that looks good. I could probably rock that, too!"

Having said that, you might want to consider selling the

concept of your items instead of just the items themselves. Case in point: The North Face. This brand focuses on outdoor gear and sporting goods, offering some of the best performing winter clothing essentials on the market. On their Facebook page, you'll notice that the central point of their posts isn't the products themselves, but the experiences that their users have had while wearing their products.

Provide a Price Range

A powerful psychological tool used across a variety of marketplaces and e-commerce platforms is the anchoring bias. It is Designed to designate the concept cheap and expensive, this psychological online selling tactic that helps encourage prospects to purchase because it shows that your items aren't all that expensive.

A basic marketing truth is that when presented with a comparison of prices, people will naturally gravitate towards the cheapest option. This helps designate an anchor, making it easier to figure out whether the more expensive choices are worth it or impractical.

Consider this: if the basic Kindle was presented as a stand-alone product without any other choices or variants next to it, do you think buyers would consider it cheap? To most, paying $79.99 for an eBook reader might be an unnecessary luxury, but because it shows you that the other choices are more expensive, you can establish a price range and determine that, after all, $79.99 isn't that expensive.

In the same light, the anchoring bias also helps to establish the value of the items being presented. Sure, $79.99 looks cheap now, but for an extra $50, you can get the Kindle Paper white which boasts a range of features that make it more appealing than the basic one. Now, when comparing the specs across the board, buyers can conclude that the second choice isn't that expensive, because it has significantly more features for just a small added cost.

Leveraging this technique on your Facebook page is as simple as posting a few extra items on your store for buyers to establish a cost. In effect, what you'd want is a side-by-side view of items spanning a wide range of prices to give your prospects a better idea of your lower and upper bounds.

Heighten the Fear (of Missing Out)

Deals and offers that last a limited amount of time increase the sense of urgency in buyers. "FREE shipping, ONLY TODAY!" Of course, shipping fees rarely ever cost a lot anyway, but just the fact that it's being offered free for a short period makes people not want to miss out on the chance, even if what they're buying isn't necessary anyway.

When seeing offers like these, especially from brands that don't do it often, a buyer's knee-jerk response would be to engage and take advantage of the deal because they might not be able to get the same perks later on, but how can you present it powerfully on your page?

Along the left-hand panel, you'll see a tab labeled "Offers." Here, you can create unique publications that give buyers promotional or discount offers that expire after a certain period. The offer gets posted as a publication on your page, featuring an image, an expiration date, and a title. If you're offering a unique promo code for your e-commerce website, you have the option to add the unique code to the offer so that users can copy it and key it in when they purchase on your web page.

When should you be giving away offers like these? For the most part, you'll want to provide promotions and discount offers at specific points in the year, such as during special holidays and seasons where demand for your products or services are high. If you're trying to get rid of old inventories before you stock up on a new line of items, you may want to offer discounts for old stocks to clear them out of your storage. Discount offers also work well to reignite interest in your brand. For instance, if you've noticed a dip in sales, you can provide a promotional discount to help generate extra traffic and drive more profitable consumer action.

Amp It Up

Creating hype around a product launch or a brand-new facet to your business can draw in more attention at the get-go to fuel more sales. One of the ways you can increase revenue with your Facebook page would be to use it to spark interest in your audience on a brand-new line of items that you're offering.

These days, the pre-launch hype is a powerful tool that many businesses use. Posts don't need to be definitive or descriptive and need to leave consumers wondering, asking questions in their heads, and marking their calendars to find out what all the hype is about. Consider how Shopee - one of Asia's largest mobile marketplaces does this.

It doesn't say anything beyond the fact that they're giving away vouchers, but the information provided is more than enough to keep prospects on the look-out for their upcoming offers. On the business's page, you'll also see that they post updates on their fast-approaching sale almost every day. This increases excitement and anticipation amongst their buyers and helps guarantee that there will be sales on the day that they finally release their discount offers and vouchers.

Facebook Groups

Groups are great for marketing, especially from a business point of view, because they allow you to interact with a highly targeted audience. People join groups only if they have a specific need, and they expect people in that group to fulfill that need. With groups, you can increase your awareness of what your customers want while at the same time directly advertising your business to them.

How to join a group?

Groups are just small communities on Facebook, and you can join over 6,000 of them. If you want to join a group, click on the Groups tab on your Facebook profile, and you'll be redirected to the Discover Groups page. On this page, you can search for different groups on the basis of keywords or find groups on the basis of your interests or the pages you've liked.

For a business, the best thing to do is to type the kind of business that you do. If you sell clothes, simply type clothes, and you'll find multiple groups with discussions and clothes recommendations.

Some groups are public, while others are private. If it's a closed group, you will have to send a join request, and you will then have to be approved by an admin. You can click on the description of a group to find out the rules of engagement, and it's better to follow these, as you might otherwise get kicked out.

Conclusion

Once again, I thank you for choosing this book and hope you had a good time reading it. The main aim of this book was to educate you on the use of Facebook for business and how you can use the social media platform to enhance your reach.

The book has extensively explained every step in marketing your business on Facebook and how you should go about it, and also how to get started with a Facebook page for your business get a firm standing for your business.

To further reinforce the concept and come up with a good marketing plan for your business, you can go through the book again. You do not need to have a Facebook profile to create a page as you can create one with a separate Facebook account. It means that you don't need to have a personal profile to open a business account)

Once you create a page, it is best to employ someone who is an expert at managing social media profiles to take care of the page.

Thank you once again for choosing this book and wish you good luck with your Facebook page. If you found the book informative, I request you to recommend the book to others who you think may benefit from the information.

References

http://www.useturbo.com/blog/facebook-advertising-audience-research

https://adespresso.com/guides/facebook-ads-beginner/demographic-targeting/

https://sproutsocial.com/insights/facebook-audience-insights/

https://buffer.com/library/how-to-create-manage-facebook-business-page

https://www.postplanner.com/how-to-improve-your-branding-on-facebook/

https://www.leadpages.net/blog/facebook-ad-lead-magnets/

https://blog.hootsuite.com/how-to-get-more-likes-on-facebook/

https://adespresso.com/guides/facebook-ads-beginner/create-first-facebook-ad/

https://buffer.com/best-time-to-post-on-facebook

https://fitsmallbusiness.com/how-to-sell-on-facebook-shop/

A message from the Author

Once again i would like to thank you for downloading this book.

Reviews are very important for an author.hence, would you be kind enough to leave a review? it will only take 1-2 minutes of your time.

An honest review will be highly appreciated.

Click on the "**Write a Customer Review button**" and post your review here.

thank you again and i look forward to having you on board our community.

Best wishes

Nadz

About the Author

Online brand supremo was built with one goal in mind. how to help anyone to start a brand and build a presence online.whether you are a business owner,employed,or retired. if you have an interest, there are millions of people out there that would love to listen to what you have to offer.

in the online space there is a lot of content that can confuse you, and get you of track.hence,the online brand supremo community i am building is for like minded people to share what actually works online and learn how to build a brand the right way. that is why we have a tag line here that says;

" Stop the Side hustle! become a supremo!" in an essence, learn how to brand build the right way.

You can connect with me on:
🌐 https://onlinebrandsupremo.com
🐦 https://twitter.com/Nadz02379585
f https://www.facebook.com/Online-Brand-Supremo-487194511803880

Subscribe to my newsletter:
✉ https://onlinebrandsupremo.com/infograph

www.ingramcontent.com/pod-product-compliance
Lightning Source LLC
Chambersburg PA
CBHW021445210526
45463CB00002B/635